# VOLUME IV

# Improving Classroom Practice Through Culturally-Transformative Teaching

*A Guide for All Teachers*

*by*

*Maxine Newsome, Ph.D.*

MODEL ALTERNATIVE SCHOOL SERVICES PROFESSIONAL DEVELOPMENT
SERIES FOR EXCELLENCE IN TEACHING AND LEARNING

*This series is dedicated to my late husband and friend, Thomas Newsome I, who was the wind beneath my wings in living through the topics and events of this series.*

Copyright © 2012 by Maxine Newsome.
*All rights reserved, including the right of reproduction in whole or in part or in any form.*
ISBN   978-0-9839496-3-3
Published by MASS

Please visit www.schoolin.org for further consultation and inquiry.

# MASS
*Professional Development Series for Excellence in Teaching and Learning*

## CONTENTS

*Volume I*

The Context of Classroom Practice in American Schools

*Volume II*

Improving Classroom Practice Through Culturally-Inclusive Classroom Management

*Volume III*

Improving Classroom Practice Through a Culturally-Centered Education Program

*Volume IV*

Improving Classroom Practice Through Culturally-Transformative Teaching

"As the editor of this book and as a licensed educator in the public school system, I have deepened my understanding of what my population of students will require for growing through their transitions in my classrooms with joy and a sense of recognition—and of how I can be the greater teacher that I have not yet had the courage to be.

We all have to learn to come from the places that others come from and to be guests in those places, and to teach to those places in ourselves while holding them open for the interactions of others. With the authority of a caring friend on the journey to genuine and masterful teaching, the work will bring your thinking as an educator in today's world to another, more encompassing platform—so that we can all enjoy these new places of beauty together."

Erjan Slavin, Teacher, Author, Poet, Editor
--Peekskill, NY

*"Building cross-cultural understanding for a caring world through excellence in classroom practice..."*

# Overview of the MASS Professional Development Series

"We can change the world!" is clearly a belief of many young people and is a major reason why many decide to enter the field of education. At no point in time has the challenge set forth in this rallying cry been more relevant than today as we look toward a Twenty-First Century world.

Now, the work begins. It involves the way that you, the teachers of America, take on this challenge through the practices that you employ in your classrooms. It has to do with your insight and ability to help students from multiple cultural backgrounds to learn, interact with each other, understand each other, and to care for and about each other.

Changing the world may seem like a lofty goal...but when you think about it, given the number of students with whom you will interact over the course of your career, you are positioned to change the lives of many. You will have students as your captive audience for more hours than any other of society's institutions, including the family. The way that you use your influence with your students in the classroom can make a lasting difference in what and how well they will learn, in their perceptions and attitudes, and in the way they will go out into the world and relate to others in the larger society. In this sense, as a classroom teacher, you can create a culturally-inclusive classroom to serve as a microcosm for building respect, understanding, and caring in a multicultural world. The power to change the society resides with you, a dedicated teacher, who nurtures your students to be the influential leaders of tomorrow. The lofty goal of changing the world will come only when you have the vision of what it can be, and acknowledge the powerful role and opportunity that you have through your teaching to improve societal conditions.

## The Cultural Dimensions of Classroom Practice

The Model Alternative School Services' *Professional Development Series for Excellence in Teaching and Learning* emphasizes culturally-compatible classroom practice as the foundation for excellence in teaching and learning. The belief expressed throughout the series is that culture is integral to the actual practices in American classrooms. The approach is to make the theory and research on effective teaching, classroom management, and multicultural education more accessible and usable by connecting it in practical ways to daily classroom practice.

The four-volume series aims to have you become what Henry Giroux refers to as a transforming intellectual. A major step in the transformation is to have you begin to learn about dominant mainstream culture—something that has been omitted in multicultural discourse. The series seeks to develop your cultural and pedagogical knowledge and competence so that you can display your developing expertise in the classroom to assure learning excellence for all of your students.

The series proposes that students be taught the dominant American mainstream culture, its manifestations and ramifications, with full understanding of why they are learning it, and how they can transform and make use of this knowledge in their lives to make a difference. In other words, students learn the dominant "culture of power" thoroughly and in depth as a means to an end, so that they have essential knowledge and insight into the dominant culture, and the willingness and readiness to change "what is" toward a more embracing international culture.

The educational content, level of critical inquiry about schooling, and classroom practice strategies developed in these four volumes are not being taught in today's K-12 classrooms nor are they being taught at the university level in the schools of education. As a result of the changing face and direction of America and the void in teacher education, this professional development series is relevant, and in fact, crucial. The series is concerned with improving classroom practice on the part of beginning as well as veteran teachers. Each volume in the series is both conceptual and practical in offering original and fresh insights that are applicable in today's classroom settings.

## Your Journey Through the Series

The complete MASS *Professional Development Series* gives you the basics in knowledge and skill to operate a culturally-inclusive classroom. Volume I sets the stage for improving classroom practice by providing information to develop your cultural competence and understanding of the cultural context of American classroom practice; Volume II outlines the necessary ingredients for structuring and managing a culturally-inclusive classroom; Volume III helps you design and implement a culturally-centered education program, and Volume IV presents a comprehensive model of culturally-transformative teaching for you to assure excellence in student learning.

After you complete the three modules in Volume I of the series, you should have a basic foundation and the requisite cultural competence for effective classroom practice. *Module One* offers some insights into why classroom practice that has an aim of building cultural understanding is needed. You learn, in *Module Two*, how American schools and classrooms came to be as they are as you hear the stories of the representative cultural groups who are the focus of the series: Native American, Latino American, Asian American, African American and Arab-Muslim American. Related to *Modules One* and *Two* is the perspective that you gain in *Module Three*, which enables you to examine schools and classrooms through a lens that you might not have considered before. This third module, which introduces you to critical pedagogy, calls for you to consider the contextual and historical information from *Modules One* and *Two* and your emerging knowledge of what goes on in classrooms in relationship to what you would like your own classroom to be. *Module Three* concludes Volume I, the cultural context of classroom practice.

The background you will gain in Volume I will be essential in your effort to improve classroom practice; therefore, if you choose to read only one of the books, this one should be your choice. If you choose other books or the complete series, the cultural context for the series as presented in Volume I is highly recommended for your initial study. After studying the three modules in this volume, you will surely be motivated to alter what you have been doing and apply what you have learned to more effectively embrace all of your students. For specific ways to improve classroom practice, you will benefit from studying the complete four-volume series. The three practical volumes will explain how to go about teaching to embrace all of your students. And, if you choose, you will have an opportunity to practice and further develop your cultural and pedagogical expertise through the professional development materials and personalized sessions with MASS consultants.

Volume II of the series gives you a thorough presentation of ways to employ culturally-inclusive practices as you manage the classroom. The four modules in Volume II take you from start to finish in designing and managing your classroom in culturally-compatible ways. In *Module One*, you learn how to set forth the core principles to formulate the attitudes and behaviors, which you and your students aim to work toward in your daily classroom interactions. It is these goals or standards for behavior that give direction to the management of your classroom. *Module Two* is considered to be the essential classroom management module of this volume. It helps you set up your classroom, induct your students into the classroom environment, and teach the procedures necessary to enable students to work together. Once the classroom is set up, you have the structure for orchestrating your classroom with style, sensitivity and caring. The material outlined in *Module Three* provides approaches for you to consider as you seek to build a caring classroom community. In spite of the foundation that you establish, and the way that you structure and orchestrate your classroom, however, there will be some instances in which you will need to assist students who, from time to time, may have difficulty meeting expectations and staying on course with he established core principles of the classroom community. You learn various ways to prevent and address student misbehavior in *Module Four*.

The educational program can be viewed as the substance of teaching and learning. Volume III of the series retains this viewpoint; however, it goes on further in using the educational program as a vehicle to promote cross-cultural understanding among diverse students and families. *Module One* helps you design and implement a culturally-centered education program and *Module Two* helps you connect the educational program to your work with families. A variety of methods for communicating with families and a comprehensive approach to involving families in their child's learning will be emphasized in *Module Two*.

Moving into the delivery of the curriculum, you have the opportunity in Volume IV to embrace multiple cultures through culturally-transformative teaching, a comprehensive systematic approach to precise teaching. Culturally-transformative teaching develops and refines your teaching skill, builds cross-cultural understanding, and assures excellence in student learning. The lesson framework and the teaching principles, as they are outlined in this volume, can form the basis for a complete school or district-wide teacher development and evaluation system. Your effective use of the framework and principles transforms dominant culture material and elevates your thinking and the thinking of your students.

Building cross-cultural understanding through effective classroom practice calls for you to dismantle old ways of doing things in your classroom, and to replace them with culturally compatible practices. Your ability to assure excellence in learning for all students depends on your cultural competence and commitment to operate from a foundation of cultural inclusiveness. Since American classrooms are held to a dominant culture model, you are sure to find yourself engaged in continuous examination of your belief system about classrooms, schools, and about society itself. Your professional and personal growth rests on your openness to questioning, challenging, and ultimately of changing what is to a more open and embracing educational program and environment. These professional development materials, in combination with the accompanying lectures, seminars, and personalized consultant services are dedicated to helping you become a thoughtful discerning teacher who is dedicated to improving classroom practice.

In many ways, I think of the material you are about to read as a memoir of my life as an educator. After an extended career in teaching and administration in urban, suburban, and rural schools and school districts, I have participated directly in teaching and guiding others through the experiences described in the four-volume series. These experiences have taken place in both mainstream and culturally-diverse settings and have also included consultant services in various geographical regions of the U.S. I have numerous stories to tell about my classroom experiences over a broad educational career—and this professional development series presents an opportunity to tell many of them. Some stories are more personal involving my son, who is an integral part of MASS—Model Alternative School Services—my precious and precocious nieces and other relatives that I have been honored to teach and watch blossom into caring competent adults. Others are stories about friends and colleagues whom I have been fortunate to learn from along the way, and students whom I have taught from elementary school to graduate school. My recollection of each experience has added to my understanding of schooling and of classroom practice.

Also, the research and authorities cited in the series are those whose writings I have known, loved, and lived with over time. Over the years, these "best practices" have served me well in my work in numerous classrooms from the kindergarten to university level and in professional development settings. Educators like me have respected and incorporated the concepts and principles of such noted authorities as Jerome Bruner, Jacob Kounin, Henry Giroux, John Goodlad, Grant Wiggins, Howard Gardner, and Madelyn Hunter in our classroom practices even in the face of more recent theories. These icons in the field of education didn't just give us new trends or speculative ideas—they gave us sound concepts and principles for practices that actually work in classrooms. These authors are referred to here as masters and their writings as classics because they still set the standard for the field. It was because of these and other influential educators that I was able get better and better at my craft and consequently to influence the learning and lives of my students. The topics that I have written about are referred to in this series as evidence-based, because they present clear evidence of how the concepts and principles expressed in the writing of these and other authorities actually work in practice.

I have learned from the experts, but I have also learned from active practical research in my own classroom and in numerous other classrooms from teachers with whom I have been fortunate to work and to learn from along the way. I want us to take this journey through the series together—and I want you to conclude that the series' approaches to classroom practice have been formulated in an accordance with sound evidence-based theory, research, and practices that have stood the test of time. Hopefully, you can benefit from my experience and avoid many of the trials and errors that overwhelmed me in my early days of teaching. Think of me as your mentor as I walk along side and speak to you telling my story as we go.

# *VOLUME IV*

## CONTENTS

Introduction to Volume IV...2

*Part One*

The Culturally-Transformative Teaching Process...13

*Part Two*

The Culturally-Transformative Teaching Model...40

*Part Three*

Culturally-Transformative Teaching as a
Professional Growth Activity...72

Appendix...93

The MASS Professional Development Series in Review...103

# Introduction to Volume IV

# Improving Classroom Practice Through Culturally-Transformative Teaching

Curriculum and teaching are the substance and process of classroom practice. Volume III explained in some detail how to expand dominant-culture curriculum to create an effective culturally-centered education program. This volume emphasizes teaching as a process to transform dominant-culture curriculum to embrace all cultures. If we are "teaching the right things in the right way," our classrooms are likely to be effective and culturally inclusive. As a process, teaching influences everything that happens in the classroom; it is the engine that makes everything go. This influence extends beyond teaching the curriculum to teaching classroom procedures, what to do when, to teaching behavior qualities, learning skills, etc.... A basic principle of this culturally-focused professional development series is, "Anything we want students to know or do, we have an obligation to teach."

Many teachers in dominant-culture classrooms may be comfortable using facilitative or indirect or instructional approaches because they believe they can assume the requisite cultural background knowledge on the part of dominant culture students, but this assumption is not valid with non-dominant culture students. For these students in particular, contextual direct thorough skilled teaching is crucial; the cultural backgrounds and learning styles of these students must also be part of the teaching equation. Their learning and the learning of all students cannot be left to chance. This volume addresses teaching as a comprehensive process in which learning excellence is the course of action which effective teachers of culturally-transformative lessons take to accomplish this level of learning for all students.

No generally accepted criteria or methodology for what makes good teaching existed when I began teaching. We all just did the best that we could to help students in a given classroom situation learn what was in the textbooks. So when asked about our teaching methodology, the typical answer would be, "It all depends." Under such circumstances teaching was left to chance, intuitive, and arbitrary. Whatever we did, for the most part, was presumed to be acceptable. The standard for what made "good teaching" was in the eye of the beholder.

It was within this environment that such influential educators and researchers as Madelyn Hunter and Barak Rosenshine introduced us to research and teaching techniques from which we began to examine our teaching and improve what we did in the classroom. For us, the teaching effectiveness research was long overdue. We joined teachers from all over the country in rallies, lectures, and seminars to learn how to teach. Teaching was truly at the forefront in schooling and the conversation all over the country was about systematic teaching. During this era, we moved away from emphasizing the personal characteristics of the teacher to define "the good teacher," to emphasizing the teaching process itself. We now had more to say about what makes good teaching than, "It all depends." What an exciting time it was! However, now that I have progressed in my thinking about teaching and learning in American classrooms, I place the teaching effectiveness models of Madeline Hunter and Barak Rosenshine exclusively in the dominant-culture category. Still, I remain grateful that both of these educators recognized the value of outlining a clearly-defined structure and process for systematic teaching, Hunter's lesson design and Rosenshine's teaching functions. It wasn't until the cognitive theory with its interest in the varying ways in which students learn and process information that we began to have insights into how teaching might look if it were broadened to include students from cultures other than the dominant American culture.

Teaching as a science with attributes that correlate with student learning seemed to be going in the right direction for a decade or so as the attention and research continued. However, before fully influencing classroom practice, we were moving away from effective research-based teaching to other means of addressing student under-achievement, involving computer technology related uses in the classroom, scripted curriculum, and other packaged programs. Many of these "newer" ventures, designed to be teacher proof, took the methods of teaching out of the hands of teachers. Under these undefined and ineffective instructional approaches, teachers and administrators were accountable for mediocre student performance which resulted from methods over which they had little control. Again, we lost our way and continued to hear on a daily basis that students, teachers, and schools were failing.

What happened? For sure, the cyclical trends in education have set priorities and diverted attention from well researched strategies, and as with many classroom practices, even the "best teaching practices" lose ground in favor of the new flavor of the season. This is why I believe it is paramount for the teachers of this and coming generations, to know the "best" research-based practices, to apply them in their classrooms, and to make sure that "new ideas" are not in conflict with them. There is general agreement that teaching is the most important function that schools and teachers do; consequently, teaching excellence must be the highest priority; that is to say, that all students will learn from and because of the teaching they receive in any one of our classrooms. Up to this point, we have not met this standard, certainly not with all student populations.

This volume is arranged in three parts. Part One explains the teaching competencies that are associated with effective culturally-transformative lessons as well as the application of the competencies in the teaching of culturally-transformative lessons. Part Two outlines the Culturally-Transformative Teaching Model, the teaching principles, performance indicators, and the process for including these elements in your lessons.

These two parts, which are addressed primarily to teachers, are activated, supported, and put into practice in Part Three, which describes a cooperative professional growth process where individual teachers and groups of teachers work together and are assisted by mentors and supervisors to develop high quality culturally-transformative lessons.

# Volume IV—Improving Classroom Practice Through Culturally-Transformative Teaching

Opening Scenario...8

Key Concepts...13

## Part One: The Culturally-Transformative Teaching Process...13

- Culturally-Transformative Teaching: What It Is, How It Builds Cross-Cultural Understanding and Assures Excellence in Student Learning...14

- Culturally Transformative Teaching: A Comprehensive Approach...16

    Direct/Explicit Teaching...16

    Cooperative Group Learning...17

    Inquiry Group Discussions...17

- Culturally-Transformative Teaching: A Summary of the Research, Theory, and Concepts...18

- The Research and Evidence-Based Teaching Competencies for Culturally-Transformative Teaching...20

    Know the Content So That You Can Examine and Shape It to Build Cross-Cultural Understanding...20

    Demonstrate the Ability to Help Students Learn and Transfer Learning to Multiple Contexts...21

    Hold and Display High Expectations for All Students...22

    Possess and Display Other Personal and Professional Qualities That Connect with All Students...23

    Understand and Build on Students' Cognitive Style in Making Teaching Decisions...24

Demonstrate the Ability to Conduct Informal Diagnosis in the Process of Teaching...24

Demonstrate the Ability to Individualize Instruction in the Process of Teaching...25

Demonstrate the Ability to Conduct Remediation During and After the Lesson...26

Demonstrate the Skill and Quality of Teaching Which Develops and Raises Students' Intellectual Ability and Instructional Levels...26

Demonstrate the Ability to Interact and Assist Students with Processing Information...27

Demonstrate the Ability to Respond to Students in Ways That Keep Them Motivated and Wanting to Excel...28

Demonstrate the Ability to Manage Time to Maximize Learning...29

Demonstrate the Ability to Manage the Instructional Environment to Promote Student Attention and Engagement in Learning...30

Demonstrate the Ability to Establish and Maintain Positive Student Behavior...30

- The Research and Evidence-Based Competencies Applied in Culturally-Transformative Lessons...31

  Introducing the Lesson, Engaging Students, and Setting the Context for the Lesson...32

  Teaching the Lesson for Content Mastery and Ongoing Learning...33

  Interacting with Students, Giving Them Directed Practice, and Encouraging Their Learning...34

  Student Accountability, Independent Practice and Assessment...35

  Transfer, Discerning Relationships and Transferring Knowledge from One Setting to Another...36

# Part Two: The Culturally-Transformative Teaching Model...40

- The Components of the Culturally Transformative Teaching Model...40

    The Teaching Principles and Performance Indicators, the Substance of Culturally-Transformative Lessons...42

    The Lesson Framework and Lesson Agenda, the Organizers of Culturally-Transformative Lessons...51

- A Model Culturally-Transformative Lesson: Using the Lesson Framework to Integrate the Teaching Principles, and Performance Indicators in the Lesson...55

- Managing Culturally-Transformative Lessons: Designing, Planning, Implementing, and Reflecting on Lessons...63

    Preparing/Designing the Lesson...64

    Developing the Lesson Plan...66

    Presenting the Lesson...67

    Implementing the Lesson...68

    Reflecting on the Lesson...69

# Part Three: Culturally-Transformative Teaching as a Professional Growth Activity...72

- Basic Premises and Beliefs Which Guide the Process...72

- The Source and Rationale for Culturally-Transformative Teaching as a Growth Process...74

- Looking Up Close at the Process...75

    The Professional Growth Sequence...75

    Gaining Proficiency in the Process...76

- The Professional Growth Process in Schools and Universities…77

    Professional Growth in School Settings…78

        Orientation Prior to the Opening of School…80

        Follow-Up and Classroom Visitations…80

        Follow Up and Classroom Visitations Continued…81

        Summary of Performance and Evaluations…81

    Professional Growth in University Settings…82

        Orientation Sessions for All Participants in the Process…84

        The Implementation Sequence in Teaching Center Schools…85

- A Call to Action…86

Classroom Teachers Talk It Over…87

A Summary of Learning in Volume IV…88

Opening Scenario (Afterthoughts)…90

Questions/Activities…90

Looking in Classrooms…91

Recommendations for Further Reading…92

## Opening Scenario

Cati Harwood, a beginning teacher in a typical modern-day American classroom, has been assigned to teach colonial life in America, as a unit of study in her culturally-diverse fifth-grade classroom. She is interested in implementing the latest pedagogical techniques, and consequently, her thoughts return to her teacher preparation program and what she learned during her methods courses. From these courses she learned to value student-initiated rather than teacher-directed learning. She concluded, therefore, that she would avoid using teacher-directed culturally- laden teaching techniques, that she would use group learning, which she read was the best method for working with culturally-diverse students, and that she would be non-directive in her instructional approach.

As she began to consider her strategy for working with the students, she decided that to keep from imposing her values on the students, she would leave everything very open-ended, believing that the students by working together would give *her* direction about what they would like to learn. She decided, therefore, to let her students work in the groups of their choice without undue direction from her. She also wanted them to make their own decisions about what they would like to work on, and how they would like to work together. She knew that she would need to be patient but, she reasoned that by giving the students latitude to figure out their strategies for themselves, she would obtain greater interest and commitment to learning from them.

It wasn't long into the process when she wondered whether her approach was working. She thought that a leader from each of the groups would emerge and that a variety of ideas would flow during the group planning session, but she soon detected confusion as she heard such comments coming from the groups as:

"What does she want us to do?"

"You might be in my group but you don't have any right to tell me what to do. You're not the teacher."

"She's the teacher who is supposed to be teaching us. Doesn't she know how to teach?"

"If I really get to choose what I want to do, then, I choose not to be in this class."

"I wish I could return to my last year's teacher. She taught us what to do and how to do it—and we did it. In fact, every time she taught a lesson, she wrote an agenda (see p. 10) on the board and then explained what we were supposed to do in the lesson."

Soon the tenor of this class changed for the worse. Students began to leave their groups to find out what other groups were doing. Some said they were going to the library to get books to give them ideas. Many students were out of their seats milling around. Students began calling each other names. This class was out of control...

*What happened here? What did the teacher do or not do?*
*How does the teacher in this scenario, in the effort to avoid being culturally biased, actually encourage such problems?*

*What perceptions do you have about teaching to build cross-cultural understanding as you begin this volume?*

*As you prepare to become or continue your role as a teacher in today's world of culturally-diverse classrooms, you may identify with this situation. Also, you may wonder what you need to do to be effective in a similar culturally-diverse classroom.*

---

The education program, discussed in Volume III, focused on diversity among students and their learning styles, planning the subject matter to be taught, and the authentic assessment of student learning. Expanding on these areas of the education program, you will see in this volume that no facet of an education program is more significant than the process used to teach what students are expected to know and be able to do. The culturally-centered education program is to be powered by culturally-transformative teaching.

This fourth volume of the MASS Professional Development Series presents a comprehensive approach to the research-based teaching of daily ongoing lessons in contextual, explicit, precise, systematic ways. Cooperative learning and issue-oriented dialog techniques, also included in the series comprehensive approach to teaching, are explained in Volume II. This volume focuses on direct whole-group teaching to serve as the background and structure to support these techniques.

*Clearly, there is no one best way to teach. Effective teaching requires teachers to have a repertoire of tools upon which to best match content, method and student. The more tools teachers have the better the teaching decisions. Expertise in conducting contextual step-by-step teaching and in conducting cooperative learning and issue-oriented discussion sessions enables teachers to best match content, method, and student.*

This series recognizes teaching as decision making defined as a science and an art, dependent upon scientific research and evidence-based practice in combination with teaching style. Teachers clearly need to have the discretion to create learning experiences to address the needs of students in their classrooms. Having this discretion, however, makes it crucial that teachers also have the teaching expertise to determine the task, the anticipated behavior of the students, and the teaching strategies that are most appropriate to ensure excellence in student learning in each given situation. It is this learned ability of combining teaching decisions with student needs which only a skilled teacher can accomplish. The teaching process and model in this volume are designed to ensure that teachers have the expertise to teach comprehensively, provide sufficient practice and review, and employ correctives as needed in the ongoing teaching effort so that all students learn regardless of their cultural backgrounds or status in American society. This volume is committed to developing this level and quality of teaching ... and more.

Culturally-transformative teaching expands on the effective teaching research by employing cognitive learning theory and evidence-based practices to also emphasize context. In brief, it calls for teachers to develop the cultural context for the lesson and relate it to student's background knowledge, teach the material from multiple perspectives, and make sure that it is learned and transfers to make real-world applications of what is learned. Teachers are called upon to teach consciously and systematically what students need to know to be successful in American society, specifically, the dominant "culture of power" but in a broader more inclusive way. Culturally-transformative teaching is the agent behind broadening the concepts associated with the dominant "culture of power" as a step in the effort to build cross-cultural understanding and excellence in student learning.

My belief in this level and quality of teaching was initiated years ago when, as a teacher and supervisor, I began to think more critically about schooling and classroom practice. Other than to follow the textbook, there seemed to be a lack of clarity in the minds of many teachers about what to do in the act of teaching and why. At points during my supervisory visits, teachers would quiet the class and just start teaching without setting the stage or attempting to make learning real or important to students. Quite the contrary, I wasn't looking for the classroom to be turned into a rain forest to teach the subject, for the teaching to mimic "Sesame Street," or for the approaches to duplicate what students do in their homes and neighborhoods for learning to be real. But clearly, the students did need a context and rationale for what they were attempting to learn that made sense to them. There was also convincing evidence that many students also found classrooms and the teaching that took place in them to be confusing. During my random visits to schools and classrooms, for example, students would respond to my queries about what they were doing by saying, "We're doing schoolwork." And, when I continued to probe, there was no coherent explanation from students about what they were doing, why, how, or to in any way suggest any significance to what was going on.

This volume responds to this need by offering, in a three-part format, a comprehensive explanation of culturally-transformative teaching. Part One offers insights into the concept, associated competencies, and a process for teaching culturally-transformative lessons. Part Two puts forth a model for teaching culturally-transformative lessons which can be used to help teachers develop and refine their skill in teaching lessons. Part Three, then, sets up a professional growth process to enable teachers and mentors to collaborate and grow in their ability to teach culturally-transformative lessons.

As you study this volume, you should focus on answering the following key questions:

- What is culturally-transformative teaching, and how does it influence cultural understanding and excellence in student learning?

- How is culturally-transformative teaching comprehensive in helping you promote excellence in student learning and build cross-cultural understanding?

- How do the key elements of the teacher effectiveness research, cognitive learning and critical pedagogy theory, and evidence-based practice contribute to competency in culturally-transformative teaching?

- What are the components of the culturally-transformative teaching model and how do these components relate to the theory, research and "best practice" in teaching.

- How are the teaching principles and performance indicators integrated in the lesson?

- How do you design, plan, implement, and reflect on lessons?

- How can the teaching model and approaches be used as a professional development activity?

## Key Concepts

set induction ~ variety ~ time ~ questioning/responding ~ probe ~ prompt ~ clarity~ monitoring ~ feedback/reinforcement ~ behavior ~ climate ~ thinking/ability ~ transfer ~ direct instruction ~ structure ~ critical attributes ~ issue-oriented dialog ~ schema ~ emancipatory ~ whole-part-whole ~ lesson outline/organizer/agenda ~ events, activities, phases ~ micro knowledge ~ macro knowledge ~ lesson alignment

# Part One: The Culturally-Transformative Teaching Process

Part One of this volume is devoted to explaining culturally-transformative teaching as a concept and process to build cross-cultural understanding and excellence in student learning. The section begins by defining culturally-transformative teaching. Then, the research and concepts upon which culturally-transformative teaching is based will be explained. From this body of knowledge, a series of research and evidence-based competencies are introduced. The five phases of teaching illustrate how the competencies interact in the process of preparing for and teaching culturally-transformative lessons. This part of the volume sets the stage for you and for teachers in general to understand the steps leading up to the teaching model in Part Two and the growth process in Part Three.

## Culturally-Transformative Teaching: What It Is, How It Builds Cross-Cultural Understanding, and Assures Excellence in Student Learning

Culturally-transformative teaching is systematic purposeful contextual teaching. Its function is to broaden students' cultural knowledge and insights in a manner that builds cross-cultural understanding and promotes excellence in their learning by engaging them intellectually and broadening their perspectives. In contrast, non-contextual dominant-culture teaching misses the mark in terms of building cross-cultural understanding and excellence in learning because it fails to acknowledge and address the thinking and learning styles of students from non-dominant cultures who have different cultural orientations and use different knowledge bases to make sense of what they are learning. It also falls short in expanding the learning opportunities for dominant-culture students as well in that it fails to lead them to other ways of thinking and being beyond the American way.

The process leading to culturally-transformative teaching for me has been developmental requiring extensive practice learning and working with others over time. My teaching experience predates the teaching effectiveness and cognitive learning renaissance. But even then, some of us believed strongly in systematic well-defined teaching, that not all students think and process information in the same way, and we wanted a process that would accomplish these goals. It was a bit later that the teaching effectiveness research and cognitive learning theory entered the scene and soon were at the forefront of teaching practice. I saw this body of knowledge as the avenue to help us teach in ways that address student diversity in thinking and learning in a systematic way.

As we look further into what cultural-transformative teaching is, it is helpful to look at it in relationship to the perspective that prevails in American classrooms. The belief of many American students, that their worldview is the center of things, is representative of dominant-culture thinking and many of the dominant-culture teaching practices of American classrooms. The dominant-culture view is easy for American students to embrace on the surface because it fits with their background experiences and assessments. As pointed out by Sonia Nieto, American students learn to think of themselves as the norm and to think of others as deviations (Nieto, 2000, p.312). Such thinking causes them to have misconceptions about other cultures and to misinterpret new information about other cultures if the information is inconsistent with their view of the world. They tend to look for information that confirms their existing beliefs and ignore disconfirming evidence (Duit, 1991; Gunstone & White, 1981; Kuhn, Amsel & O'Loughlin, 1988).

When students hold these misconceptions about other cultures, the world and their place in it, teachers must help them revise their thinking. A revision in the thinking of dominant-culture students is more likely to happen through culturally-transformative teaching where misconceptions can be identified, beliefs challenged, and the pros and cons of various explanations pointed out. Multiculturalists believe that it is important to help students realize that there are several equally valid interpretations of any single event (Banks, 1991). Culturally-transformative teaching is designed to broaden the way both dominant and non-dominant culture students interpret learning experiences.

Culturally-transformative teaching responds to the intellectual and societal needs of both dominant and non-dominant culture students. For non-dominant culture students, it teaches the dominant "culture of power," the knowledge and skills that are essential to living in American society, as a step in the transformation toward cross-cultural understanding. At the same time, it addresses the misconceptions of dominant-culture students in a way that moves these students toward a broader reality. The culturally-transformative teaching process critically examines dominant-culture material within a world-wide context and enables dominant-culture students to consider their past learning experiences in light of the new evidence within this broader context. In contrast to open-ended approaches, culturally-transformative teaching leaves little to chance irrespective of students' backgrounds.

Culturally-transformative teaching broadens student thinking about other cultures in relationship to dominant-culture knowledge. It focuses on meaningful general knowledge and its relationship to the knowledge that students already possess—their cultural and individual background knowledge. It calls for teachers to recognize that there are multiple ways to learn, to connect new information to each student's ***schema*** (background or existing networks of prior knowledge), to continuously build connections and differing perspectives among points of learning, and to integrate new learning with each student's cultural background experiences. The process encourages the student to elaborate and question, add new elements, and build new knowledge structures. As new information is provided, each student constructs his or her own unique meaning within the context of his or her cultural background and experiences.

Through culturally-transformative teaching, students have opportunities to process and apply their knowledge to solve problems that affect their lives and the lives of the world's peoples. Typically, schools and classrooms have the responsibility for socializing students to adjust to American mainstream societal norms. This professional development series is concerned with broadening these societal norms. Culturally-transformative teaching, with its well-defined structure and process can play a substantial role in societal change. It makes no assumptions about what students should have learned as part of their socialization in their family settings or in schools and society. The belief is that *teachers should teach explicitly all that students are expected to know and be able to do*, in both the academic and affective realms.

# Culturally-Transformative Teaching:
# A Comprehensive Approach

Culturally-transformative teaching is contextual teaching that obtains meaning from the bigger picture—from whole to part, system to event. It is generic, applicable to all subject matter and grade levels K-12 and beyond, and it embraces multiple teaching and learning styles. In this series there is a narrowed focus on the lesson because it is at this micro level that teaching can most effectively be taught, observed, analyzed, and improved. This volume is concerned with the way that lessons are taught, learned, and transferred to broader contexts beyond the classroom.

## Direct/Explicit Teaching

Culturally-transformative teaching is direct/explicit teaching; however, it also includes as sub-components cooperative learning, issue oriented dialog, and other interactive approaches. Direct/explicit teaching calls for conscious, active, and precise teaching of the intellectual skills, subject matter, classroom management tasks, and other complementary learning processes. It requires teachers to play a significant and direct role in structuring and negotiating student understandings. The lesson framework, discussed in Part Two of this volume provides the structure for his type of ***direct instruction***.

Direct instruction is also used to ensure that students receive sufficient background and support to engage in less-direct approaches during the interactive processing segment of the lesson, as members in cooperative group and in issue-oriented dialogue sessions. These forms of group learning are variations of the three broad categories of teaching, didactic, coaching of skills, and Socratic-type discussions recommended by Mortimer Adler in the Paideia Proposal (1982). Cooperative learning and issue-oriented dialog forms of group learning are discussed in Volume II of this series as features of classroom orchestration in an interactive classroom community.

## Cooperative Group Learning

Cooperative learning is included here to show how it fits into culturally-transformative lessons. Cooperative group learning is valued for its contribution to promoting harmonious relationships between students of different cultures and for creating the forum to foster interdependence in learning among heterogeneous groups of students. Two functions of cooperative learning in culturally-transformative lessons is to give students the opportunity to work together to practice and coach each other on previously taught skills, and to interpret their experiences and construct their own knowledge by creating something that is uniquely their own. In culturally-transformative teaching, cooperative coaching and collective knowledge construction *take place during the interactive phase of the direct instruction lesson after students have received sufficient background and direction from the teacher to engage meaningfully in these interactive experiences.*

## Inquiry Group Discussions

A very high premium is given to conscience raising and to proposing ways to take action on the important world issues of the day. ***Issue-oriented dialog*** sessions in a modified Socratic-type format are therefore part of teaching culturally-transformative lessons. This level of critical pedagogy dialog encourages students to see ethnocentric bias, to discuss dominant culture topics and issues, and to formulate multiple understandings on issues. Again, these *discussions are to occur as part of the interactive segment of the direct instruction lesson after students have studied the material and received sufficient instruction on the topics or issues under consideration for discussion.*

In the discussion on the Culturally-Centered Education Program in Volume III of this series, the point is made that many curriculum theorists and developers are now using the unit as the source from which teachers are to plan and carry out instructional activities. For example, when studying a unit such as the Civil War, some students may be given the choice to study the causes, others the battles…etc. with the teacher serving as a resource. When this happens teachers abdicate their role in thoroughly planning and teaching the essential "Big Ideas" associated with the war and, instead become mere facilitators of what students choose to learn. In such instances where students are engaged primarily in choosing what they learn and how they learn it, learning outcomes are often inadequate and imprecise. Students are likely to end up engaging in activities, "doing stuff" to complete the goals of the unit rather than in learning significant concepts and principles through well planned lessons. Learning derived from students' participation in unit-based activities such as these is left to chance, and when students "fall through the cracks" teachers are never quite sure what happened, where students got off-track in the learning progression.

As we consider culturally-transformative teaching in greater detail, you will be able to see that your direct involvement in conceptualizing and structuring the learning process has a major influence on the extent to which student excellence in learning the major skills and concepts, specifically those associated with cross-cultural understanding are attained. The unit is to be the larger source from which well-crafted lessons are conceived, designed, and taught.

## Culturally-Transformative Teaching: A Summary of the Research, Theory, and Concepts

Many different instructional strategies may have merit—discovery learning, computer assisted instruction, class discussions, etc., depending on the circumstances. This professional development series, however, is concerned with explicit, clear, and concise research-based teaching. The body of knowledge which stems from the research on teaching includes patterns of teaching skills and strategies that influence student behavior and learning. The research, which began during the 1970's, looked at a number of variables such as direct instruction, academic focus, and climate, and involved such researchers as (Rosenshine 1983), (Brophy 1982), (Berliner 1980), and (Evertson 1982) to name a few. Their findings provided a more scientific basis for classroom practice and the foundation for subsequent research. Much of this research has been explained and made applicable to the teaching of a lesson by Donald Cruickshank, Deborah Jenkins, and Kim Metcalf, in their book, *The Act of Teaching* (2007). Following is a list and explanation of nine of the teacher effectiveness variables discussed in their book. The remaining two variables are informed by cognitive learning theory:

1. ***Set induction*** introduces and provides a context and framework for lessons.
2. ***Variety*** keeps students interested and actively involved in lessons.
3. ***Time***, used as a facilitating parameter, controls, increases, and enhance student's opportunity for learning.
4. ***Questioning and Responding*** engages students in learning, keeps them involved, and gives all students an equal opportunity to participate in the lesson.
5. ***Clarity*** involves organizing and teaching content logically and so that it is obvious to students.
6. ***Monitoring*** gauges students' performance and assists them during teaching.
7. ***Feedback and Reinforcement*** gives students information about their progress and improves student motivation.
8. ***Positive behavior/decorum*** explains and sets the parameters for student interaction during the lesson.
9. ***Positive climate*** communicates acceptance, respect, warmth, caring, and genuine regard for students.

10. ***Developing students' thinking and ability*** concerns accessing student's cognitive abilities to identify and solve problems.

11. ***Transfer*** involves the ability to take knowledge from one situation and use it in another.

The teaching effectiveness research confirmed that what a teacher does in the classroom has an effect on student behavior and learning. In its most recent form the focus has been on the cognitive processes of *understanding and application;* that is, teachers have students learn not only the individual elements of content, but they also have students consider the context of the material and the reasons for learning it, so that they can explain it, access it, and make use of it in multiple contexts both in and outside of school (Brophy 1987), (Bruer 1993), (Perkins 1992 & Resnick 1987).

In addition to the role of the teacher, constructivist-oriented cognitive psychologists such as Duffy & Cunningham 1996 and Resnick & Klopfer 1989 have also considered the role of the student in learning. Constructivist-oriented cognitive psychologists believe there are many ways to help students construct a richer more sophisticated knowledge base such as when teachers use hands-on manipulative materials, explain how facts, concepts and ideas are interrelated, and allow students to work together to experiment and construct meaning from their experiences.

The work associated with cognitive and constructivist-oriented psychologists, in concert with teacher effectiveness researchers, and critical pedagogy theorists such as (Giroux 1988) and (McLaren 2007) have contributed to the design and elements of culturally-transformative teaching as outlined in this volume. The teaching competencies, which are extracted from this research, ultimately became the components (the teaching principles and performance indicators) of the culturally-transformative teaching model.

Teaching is all about making connections. Henry Giroux uses the terms macro and micro to discuss classroom learning in terms of the ends it serves. In this respect, teachers need to consciously and continuously help students make the connections between their ***micro knowledge***, what they learn in school, and ***macro knowledge***, related to their lives outside of the classroom. Micro objectives are the course of study or lesson objectives that make up a given subject, the means to the end. Macro objectives are the end result, the transfer and broader application of knowledge in the real world. Macro knowledge is more philosophical; it calls for students to constantly question what they are learning. Culturally-transformative teaching asks teachers to begin and develop each lesson with the question, "Why are we learning this?" constantly pursued and answered and then to conclude each lesson with the question, "For what end?" As such, each lesson becomes meaningful in terms of its application beyond the classroom. Knowledge should provide students with a sense of unity and logic that allows them to consider the implications of what they are taught. Culturally transformative teaching is geared to achieving this outcome by connecting micro and macro objectives. Learning becomes culturally transformative and ***emancipatory*** when it is able to free students from the constraints of the dominant culture.

You will have an opportunity to obtain insights into the substance and process of culturally-transformative teaching in the next section. Culturally-transformative teaching is dependent on both cultural competence and pedagogical competence. The competencies will be set forth as crucial pedagogical capabilities which teachers should possess and be able to demonstrate in the act of teaching to build cross-cultural understanding and obtain excellence in student learning.

# The Research and Evidence-Based Teaching Competencies for Culturally-Transformative Teaching

The information in this section addresses the attitudes, thought processes, and teaching qualities that are associated with teaching competency in culturally-transformative lessons. It makes use of the relevant research, learning theory, and evidence-based practice to set forth the abilities which culturally and pedagogically competent teachers demonstrate when preparing for and conducting "on your feet" culturally-transformative teaching. The managerial competencies, time management for example, are also discussed in Volume II, *Improving Classroom Practice through Culturally-Inclusive Classroom Management*. They are included here to reinforce their importance in teaching lessons.

The identified competencies do not address methodology that is unique to specific content, nor are they exhaustive in terms of addressing teaching in all contexts. Nonetheless, they are the generic competencies associated with teaching methodology in general and, in particular, the teaching qualities and processes that are fundamental to culturally-transformative teaching. They are the qualities and abilities which teachers of effective culturally-transformative lessons exhibit. This section begins by explaining the first competency, the ways in which teachers of effective culturally-transformative lessons treat the substance and content, what is to be taught in the lesson.

## Know the Content So That You Can Examine and Shape it to Build Cross-Cultural Understanding

The curriculum and instructional elements and strategies associated with building cross-cultural understanding are rarely covered in the educational literature. Teachers of effective culturally-transformative lessons rely heavily on the information and ideas expressed in this series. The MASS Professional Development Series looks into the content of culturally-transformative lessons in several ways. The foundation for understanding the issues is developed in Volume I, *The Cultural Context of Classroom Practice in American Schools* and the process for broadening the content that students learn in American schools is explained in Volume III, *Improving Classroom Practice through a Culturally-Centered Education Program*. In this volume, the instructional competencies build on insights from these two volumes. It incorporates the understandings obtained from multicultural and critical pedagogy theorists in concert with curriculum and effective teaching research and best evidence-based practices to broaden dominant-culture content.

Effective teachers of culturally-transformative lessons demonstrate four qualities that contribute to helping them expand dominant-culture curriculum. First, they have an interest in and general knowledge of the world and its peoples. Second, they are aware of the differing perspectives which those who are not included in the American story may have toward the content taught in American classrooms. A third quality is they recognize that this world knowledge needs to be taught to students to alter and extend the "America only" version of knowledge and events. A fourth, and the quality most relevant to culturally-transformative teaching, is that they have the ability to teach in ways that help students form multiple perspectives on the America-only story and use their enhanced understanding to make sense of the world.

## Demonstrate the Ability to Help Students Learn and Transfer Learning to Multiple Contexts

Teachers of effective culturally-transformative lessons build a context for the subject matter at the outset of lessons and at the end they reestablish the context and enable students to transfer and apply their new learning in other contexts. This process of whole-part-whole contextual teaching, which is the essence of transfer, calls for the teachers to assess student background knowledge in relation to the content to be taught. After this quick assessment, teachers provide the relevant information to fill in gaps in student knowledge as they build a broader knowledge base and cultural perspective, a process that continues throughout the lesson as students add to their cross-cultural knowledge and understanding.

Transfer, the ability to obtain and use knowledge and understandings in multiple contexts, is at the heart of learning and what this professional development series is all about. The professional development series and this volume in particular recognize that teachers cannot create a separate lesson for everything students need to know, nor should they. Consequently, transfer is a built-in feature of culturally-transformative lessons. Teachers who are effective teachers of culturally-transformative lessons create transferrable lessons with broad applications, they help students see relationships and build connections among points of learning, and they help students apply their knowledge in multiple contexts both in school learning and in real-world situations. Effective teachers of culturally transformative lessons use every teaching opportunity to make connections to students' lives and expand their worlds.

## Hold and Display High Expectations for All Students

Teacher expectations, a key quality from the teacher effectiveness research, colors all aspects of teaching. This variable has been researched extensively with the recognition that teachers' differential expectations are often related to students' cultural backgrounds. For example, teachers have been found to hold higher expectations for students in suburban schools serving mostly dominant-culture students, as compared to students from non-dominant cultures who most often attend urban schools. This research has also shown that high teacher expectations for student success produced more and better teaching and learning, while low teacher expectations resulted in less and lower quality teaching and learning (Good and Brophy, 2000).

Teachers of effective culturally-transformative lessons know that what teachers expect, whether in academics, behavior, or attitudes, students are likely to learn or not learn. They know that while they may not always be aware of it, their actions send messages about their expectations of students through behaviors such as the following:

- The warmth and acceptance they convey to the student through encouragement and support, assistance and help, eye contact, smiles, proximity, etc.
- The amount and quality of praise they accord to student responses.
- The amount of teaching students receive.
- The extent and degree of content coverage that students receive.
- The number of times students are called on during questioning.
- The amount of time and reassurance a student is given during questioning before calling on another student or giving the correct answer themselves.

They are aware that a tragic result of low teacher expectations is that students obtain a sense of futility about learning and can internalize a sense of hopelessness, that no matter what they do, they cannot succeed, that their efforts do not make a difference.

Teachers of effective culturally-transformative lessons understand the research on teacher expectations and make every effort to incorporate this research into their teaching. They have the attitude that *all of my students can and will learn from me and because of me.* The teachers, therefore, structure and teach lessons so that all of their students are successful and perceive themselves as valued and capable.

# Possess and Display Other Personal and Professional Qualities That Connect with All Students

Beyond teacher expectations, research points to some other personal and professional qualities that maximize teachers' ability to make positive connections with students from multicultural backgrounds as they plan for and conduct culturally-transformative lessons. A few of the competencies include being knowledgeable, having an orientation toward student success, projecting a credible professional demeanor, and organizational ability.

Teachers of effective culturally-transformative lessons are knowledgeable about the subjects they teach. They know and are able to teach the structure of their discipline (the big ideas associated with their subject matter) and its critical attributes in an expanded culturally-enriched manner. Instead of focusing mainly on teaching content, however, teachers who are effective in teaching culturally-transformative lessons are also able to manage the content so that students learn it. The teachers, for example, are able to conduct a task analysis of the curriculum to determine the "big ideas" that are at the heart of the discipline, and organize it so that it can be presented in the most efficient and effective manner to the students. Outlining the lesson sequentially in the form of a lesson agenda, which contains the lesson objective and the sequence, steps, or phases of the lesson, is an essential tool in the repertoire of these teachers.

The teachers believe that all students can learn the material and that they have the ability to teach so that all students learn it. They build on students' strengths and they strive to instill students' confidence in their abilities. In this manner, they recognize effort and potential, not just correct answers. Students feel that the tasks teachers assign are relevant and important and that they can count on their teachers to help them succeed.

Teachers of effective culturally-transformative lessons are businesslike, task and goal oriented and they convey seriousness of purpose. They establish clear and specific objectives, communicate them to students and they teach in ways that systematically and efficiently move students toward achieving the lesson objective. During teaching, they are deliberate, concise, thorough, and exact and they attend to the learning needs of all students during the lesson.

Organization is a high priority for teachers who are effective in teaching culturally-transformative lessons. They value structure, and they seek to develop these qualities in their students. They are able to see the big picture, but are also detail oriented. That is, instead of visualizing only the whole task, they also see the parts and how the parts combine in the whole task. They are able to break a task into its component parts, and then synthesize the parts to create a coherent whole. This level of analytical thinking and organizational skill are essential to contextual whole-part-whole culturally-transformative teaching.

## Understand and Build on Students' Cognitive Style in Making Teaching Decisions

Cognitive style, characterized in this volume of the series as field dependent and field independent, is discussed in detail in Volume III, *the Culturally-Centered Education Program,* as being a major contributor to understanding student differences in style of thinking and learning. Teachers of effective culturally-transformative lessons understand and apply their knowledge of cognitive style to help them to decide what approaches to take in teaching lessons. To review briefly, in field-dependent cognitive styles students tend to benefit from holistic learning situations that are embedded in context, and in field-independent learning styles students tend to benefit from sequential learning which focuses on detail and analysis.

They are similarly mindful that cognitive style is also closely related to information processing involving the right and left sides of the brain, where the right side more quickly grasps the whole context and the left side is more logical, detail oriented, and amenable to a step-by-step approach. The teachers, for example, are informed that according to Baloche (1998) European American students tend to be more field independent (able to respond to non-contextual learning segments) and Latin American, Native American, and African American students tend to be more field dependent (responsive to learning segments when placed in context). And, as referenced in Volumes I-III of this professional development series, teachers of effective culturally-transformative lessons are aware but skeptical about dominant-culture students being able to learn dominant-culture material without having a context for it based on the presumption that students already possess the requisite the cultural background knowledge for learning dominant-culture concepts from their homes and societal backgrounds.

Teachers of effective culturally-transformative lessons take the apparent cultural differences of dominant and non-dominant cultures into account but are interested most in designing lessons to compliment the cognitive styles of both cultures. Therefore, learning segments are placed in context and taught sequentially so that learning is enhanced for both dominant and non-dominant culture students.

## Demonstrate the Ability to Conduct Informal Diagnosis in the Process of Teaching

Teachers of effective culturally-transformative lessons are able to determine where students are in relationship to what they plan to teach. They are aware that diagnosis of student abilities can occur through both formal and informal means. However, they know that using formal pencil and paper tests to determine where new learning is to begin fails to capture the dynamic nature of teaching a lesson. They know that *informal diagnosis is the heart and core of culturally-transformative teaching,* that it is easy to obtain and is available at the moment it is needed in teaching decisions. By making informal diagnosis at the beginning of lessons in such ways as asking questions to assess student background knowledge on the topic to be taught, teachers obtain an assessment of what students already know. By being vigilant through questioning and observing, teachers decide the extent to which they need to build student background knowledge before proceeding, and at any point in the lesson whether to move on or go back and re-teach.

In addition to diagnosis to determine student ability an often overlooked need is for teachers to determine the effort students are willing to expend. Learning effort takes into account willingness to persevere, motivation, distractibility, and previous experience. A student who may be viewed initially as marginal student may be so motivated if the material is seen as having particular relevance that learning for that student is efficient, and a bright student so unmotivated if the material is perceived as not having relevance that maximum effort is required to engage the student in learning. Teachers of effective culturally-transformative lessons consider the complexity of content to be sure that it is interesting and motivating, and accommodates for student variability in both ability and effort.

## Demonstrate the Ability to Individualize Instruction in the Process of Teaching

How to meet individual student needs in a diverse classroom has been a perennial instructional problem, often taken to mean each student working on something different using workbooks or computers to serve as the source of instruction or setting up homogeneous ability groups within the class or school. With the presence of increased cultural diversity, such arrangements are sure to be intensified. However, these approaches have proven to be dubious at best and destructive at worst. With teachers attempting to juggle so many learning situations and with students receiving little direct instruction from the teacher, it is obvious that learning is more likely to be diminished rather than enhanced. When individualization of student learning is viewed and carried out in classrooms in this manner, the professional responsibility and decision making role of the teacher to successfully teach a heterogeneous group of students have been relinquished.

Individualization of instruction in the context of a whole-group lesson can be challenging and it does take skill and sensitivity but it is doable and teachers of effective culturally-transformative lessons strive to meet this challenge. Their ability to address varying student needs within a group format requires *knowing the students, knowing the subject matter, and knowing how to conduct deliberate precise teaching to assure content mastery by all students.* The level of skill necessary to meet this challenge is explained throughout this volume.

Determining the extent of practice that is appropriate for students to solidify and retain what they have learned is also an important individualization criterion of effective culturally-transformative teaching. Frequent practice is particularly important in the early grades and with non-dominant culture students who may be coming in contact with the instructional material for the first time. Teachers of effective culturally-transformative lessons know that it may take a number of repetitions until students are firm in their understandings of content and quick and accurate in their skill development. They also know that student practice to reach this threshold is important for such a foundation stimulates confidence and enables students to believe in their abilities going forward.

## Demonstrate the Ability to Conduct Remediation During and After the Lesson

The teaching mindset for effectiveness in teaching culturally-transformative lessons is to be precise and thorough in teaching the *key objectives—the broad and general principles* that are essential to students' ongoing success in the educational program, to know which students are likely to need more help at the outset of lessons, and to take special care throughout the lesson to attend to the learning needs of these struggling students. Yet, even when teachers are diligent and successful in carrying out the teaching functions outlined in this section, some students still may need more help.

A promising approach which teachers of effective culturally-transformative lessons contemplate is derived from the mastery learning method for handling student diversity in lessons. In this method teachers deliver the same lesson and assessment to all students, but incorporate expansion activities for more capable students, and thus allow more time and assistance for students who need it. The teacher's goal in remediation is to provide intensive tutorial instruction to struggling students to enable them to keep pace with the class. Accelerated learning approaches which stress the critical learning attributes (key ideas) of the instructional material are emphasized at this point rather than extensive drill and practice on sub-skills. Effective remediation requires the teachers to tune in to the students' cognitive styles and to strive for mastery until student learning of the essential learning objectives is firm.

## Demonstrate the Skill and Quality of Teaching Which Develops and Raises Students' Intellectual Ability and Instructional Levels

Teachers of effective culturally-transformative lessons are also concerned with students' intellectual development; that is, with raising students' instructional level by developing students' thought processes through systematic teaching. This is done by bringing the students' mental processes to the surface through metacognition, a process discussed more extensively in Volume III. In metacognition students are taught to think out loud about their thinking, explain how they arrived at certain conclusions and where appropriate, be lead toward more productive ways to think through situations.

Intellectual development for teachers of effective culturally-transformative lessons is also augmented by employing holistic and multisensory learning approaches. Students are taught to formulate concepts and generalizations rather than to simply learn isolated bits of information and they aim for depth in understanding over breadth and surface learning. The teaching strategies contain the three sensory channels (visual, auditory, and kinesthetic) and address cognitive style. Essentially, as an increasing number of cognitive processes take their rightful place in the repertoire of teachers of culturally-transformative lessons, the students' instructional level simply becomes a point of reference to be constantly adjusted upward.

## Demonstrate the Ability to Interact and Assist Students with Processing Information

Teachers of effective culturally-transformative lessons keep students mentally alert by developing their lessons to engage students' intellectual processes. When students are engaged and teaching is highly interactive, teachers instill in the minds of students that they are there to assist, but that it is the students who are responsible for learning. Since high achieving classrooms are characterized by a high level of student involvement, teachers seek to sustain student involvement throughout the lesson.

The teachers of effective culturally-transformative lessons display skill in involving students through the questions they ask and in responding to the answers students give. This skill comes into play during the interactive phase of lessons when teachers are seeking both quantity through high student participation rates and quality through students' thoughtful responses. The teachers, therefore, ask a high proportion of easy questions interspersed with challenging questions and they alert students to the questioning process and the expectation they have of students in response to the questions.

As an example of alerting students to the questioning process for directed questions, this is what a teacher of effective culturally-transformative lessons would be likely to tell the students: "In our lesson today I will be inviting you to answer questions by randomly calling on you by name so please be ready." By cueing students in advance students know what is expected of them and how they should participate. Teachers of effective culturally-transformative lessons are able to raise involvement levels through such directed questions by calling on students without waiting for them to raise their hands. Directed questions are considered when there is the potential for a high proportion of non-respondents in the group. They are then to be interspersed with indirect questions as students recognize the need to stay involved.

Another effective strategy which teachers of effective culturally-transformative lessons use is to ask open-ended questions, direct them to the entire group and use wait time (30 seconds or so) to allow all students to internalize the question and prepare an answer. After most or all students have raised their hands to signal their readiness to respond, the teacher calls on a volunteer whose involvement would maximize the level of group participation and the individual student's self-esteem. When wait time is employed, the teachers give students time to think and therefore the likelihood of getting better more thoughtful responses is increased.

Other useful ways the teachers use to generate thoughtful, high quality student responses are to have students respond on scratch paper or chalkboards before answering out loud or tell a partner before telling the large group. Still other techniques they use to obtain a high level of involvement are signal responses and choral or unison responses. Unison responses are often used with young children, or to reinforce points that have been learned to generate excitement in the group. For example, the teacher would say, "Now class, let's say it out loud."

The essential point in giving students so many ways to contribute in the lesson is the recognition by teachers of culturally-transformative lessons that during the interactive phase of lessons is that it is not useful to call on only a few students while other students remain non-participants. A highly interactive lesson is dynamic and exciting and students are eager to learn. When each student contributes and participates, the learning of all students is enhanced.

Teachers of effective culturally-transformative lessons ask both process and product questions. Process questions ask students to explain how they arrived at an answer or conclusion and product questions call for students to provide the right answer. In addition to developing student thought processes overall, they find it useful to ask process questions when a new concept is being introduced. By listening to students' explanations, teachers can diagnose and clarify inappropriate assumptions and help students modify their thought processes.

## Demonstrate the Ability to Respond to Students in Ways That Keep Them Motivated and Wanting to Excel

The science and art of teaching clearly combine when acknowledging students' responses during lessons. This is where teachers of effective culturally-transformative lessons expectations and beliefs in student success are demonstrated in practice. *It is important for teachers to build for student success, to structure the conditions during interactive exchanges so that students get things "right" and earn positive reinforcement or praise.* For praise to be effective, though, it must be earned, appropriate, and noticeable. During discussions and questioning activities, teachers of effective culturally-transformative lessons demonstrate support to students by using their ideas in the following ways: acknowledging the response by repeating it out loud to the class, comparing it to significant points in the learning, and summarizing the responses of several students and using them to make a point or draw a conclusion. By using student responses in these ways, learning is highly interactive as students engage with the material, the teacher, and their peers. Praise, therefore becomes noticeable and motivating as students sense their importance in the occurrence of classroom events.

Teachers of effective culturally-transformative lessons give continuous meaningful feedback and reinforcement to keep students motivated, interested, and progressing in the learning sequence. They display sensitivity when giving students feedback, however, for they know that a student's self-esteem is on the line each time the student volunteers an answer or response, particularly in a group situation. A basic rule they apply when dealing with a student's inaccurate response is that *the teacher does not leave the student until a correct response has been given by either the student or teacher. For reasons that are obvious, the teacher does not call on another student to supply the answer, "to help the student out."*

Some methods which teachers of effective culturally-transformative lessons use to handle a student's incorrect response is to rephrase the question, provide some form of re-teaching, supply additional information and clues, probe the students response and shape it toward the correct answer, and when it is clear that a correct answer is not forthcoming, the teacher supplies the answer and moves on. *Above all, the teachers find a way to dignify the student's response and effort.* They know that the ways in which they handle student responses and provide feedback to students about the appropriateness of their answers are critical to the students' learning. They, therefore, conduct their lessons so that students feel free to take risks and venture forth answers and know that their efforts are valued, that mistakes are integral to learning. The teachers' respect and concern for each student as an individual, appreciation of diversity, and emphasis on student accomplishment in a safe orderly environment, contribute to an overall sense of student well-being.

## Demonstrate the Ability to Manage Time to Maximize Learning

Time is the instructional variable that is within each teacher's domain to control. Proper use of time in the classroom depends on careful advanced planning, consistent management, focused instruction, and careful modeling—competencies which teachers of effective culturally-transformative lessons make every effort to demonstrate.

Teachers of effective culturally-transformative lessons are aware of the issues associated with time use in lessons. For example, an issue which many teachers can face in lessons is running out of time. Another is that the actual time spent in academic instruction can be less than planned or intended. If students are sent to work in small groups, for example, time is lost in the transition as students move to new locations. Materials distribution, misplaced materials, interruptions, student misbehavior, and so on... intrude on the time allocated for instruction. The teachers of effective culturally-transformative lessons take special care to address these management issues and they avoid time lost in other areas as well.

The handling of transitions, giving directions, and maintaining momentum throughout the lesson are some of the competencies that teachers of effective culturally-transformative lessons use to manage time effectively during the lesson. For instance, in giving directions, the teachers analyze the tasks involved and plan the procedures they wish students to follow in advance. Handling transitions effectively is closely related to teachers' ability to give directions and both are used effectively by the teachers to maintain momentum during the lesson. Also, teachers of effective culturally-transformative lessons are capable of overlapping, of doing more than one thing at a time as in the case of helping one student while maintaining the attention of the whole group, for this is one of the qualities cited by Kounin (1970) as an important quality of effectiveness that applies in the multifaceted dynamic process of managing lessons.

## Demonstrate the Ability to Manage the Instructional Environment to Promote Student Attention and Engagement in Learning

Teachers of effective culturally-transformative lessons set up the learning environment to promote student learning. The arrangement of student desks is crucial to student attention during the lesson. Students face the teacher during the lesson so that teachers can have direct eye contact with students and students can also have eye contact with the teacher. In this manner, there can be rapport between teacher and student. Students' eyes and facial expressions can communicate their attention and feelings about the lesson and teachers can see directly when students are confused, eager, disinterested, etc.

The teachers recognize that arrangements in which students face each other or sit with their backs to the teacher during lessons encourage inattention and disruptions. Attention getters for many of the teachers which support the eye contact criterion are, "All eyes on me, please!" "Is everyone with me?"

Also, teachers of effective culturally-transformative lessons are aware that *they* are the *key variable* in the learning environment. Therefore, they facilitate student attention and decorum by displaying a calm, firm, caring, and consistent manner and by serving as a model for students to emulate in voice quality, movement, warmth, and demeanor.

## Demonstrate the Ability to Establish and Maintain Positive Student Behavior

Teachers of effective culturally-transformative lessons develop and maintain positive student behavior by setting precise expectations for behavior when they introduce the lesson and by acknowledging appropriate behavior during the lesson. They model caring and support to all students and they foster student pride—the students' desire to be part of an orderly predictable learning environment. For teachers of effective culturally-transformative lessons, the key to positive student behavior is the teachers' expectations and the consistency with which expectations are upheld. In addition, it is the actions taken by the teachers before a problem arises that controls the level of decorum and separates effective from ineffective teachers in managing culturally-transformative lessons.

The control and stability of the lessons of teachers who are effective in teaching culturally-transformative lessons rest on the expectations they establish, the extent to which they insist on compliance with the expectations, and the ways in which they meet each challenge until the limits are accepted as the norm. The teachers know that when they allow some misbehavior to go unchallenged or when they vary their interventions according to the mood they're in, students will test the limits and when they ignore misbehavior, students soon control the lesson.

Teachers of culturally-transformative lessons create a positive learning climate where they have few distractions and behavior problems and when they do, they respond to the infractions firmly, immediately, and without harsh action. The key is they convey a calm, firm, consistent manner—that interruptions to lessons are unacceptable.

The competencies outlined in this section are certainly not conclusive; however, they are a good start toward the development of essential cultural and pedagogical competencies that are essential to culturally-transformative teaching. When you learn and employ the competencies in your lessons, and make them a part of your teaching repertoire, student learning will be increased substantially. In the next section, you will be able to see how the competencies in this section interact in the teaching of a complete lesson.

## The Research and Evidence-Based Teaching Competencies Applied in Culturally Transformative Lessons

This section illustrates the ways in which the competencies which derive from the teacher effectiveness research, cognitive learning theory, and evidence-based practice can be applied with a group of diverse students in a whole group culturally-transformative lesson. It explains the thinking and behaviors that are involved in the complex act of teaching as they would occur in the flow of a complete lesson. The thought processes and the decisions needed to assure the most effective learning outcomes for students are pointed out.

The competencies which teachers of effective culturally-transformative lessons possess as outlined in the previous section are discussed here as they would occur in five key stages of a culturally-transformative lesson: (1) introducing the lesson, engaging students and setting the context for the material to be learned; (2) teaching the lesson, providing information, in ways that aid content mastery and ongoing learning; (3) interacting with students, giving directed practice on the content, and encouraging their learning; (4) holding students accountable, having them demonstrate their learning; and (5) transfer of learning, enabling students to see relationships and transfer knowledge from one setting to another. *The aim in each lesson is to extend student thinking and learning—to add to what students knew prior to the lesson.*

## Introducing the Lesson, Engaging Students, and Setting the Context for the Lesson

The way that the culturally-transformative lesson is introduced is crucial to its success. Promoting mental readiness for what is to come generally occurs during the first few minutes of the lesson and, depending upon the subject matter to be covered, the process can be more or less dramatic, but in any event it needs to be brief and start only when students are attentive and ready.

At this stage, the concern is with setting up the lesson so that students are ready to participate and learn so it is important for teachers to be very precise, concise, and businesslike in the directions that are given. They need to discuss seating, arrangement of books and papers on desks, and the expected behavior in sufficient detail for the students, and explain why these particulars are important to their learning. It is also at this point that expectations for student participation in the lesson are also to be set.

The most critical aspect of teaching effective culturally-transformative lessons occurs at this point in the introduction as the context for the lesson is established. When the context for the lesson is determined, students know how this segment of learning fits into a broader world-wide context. Since most of what is learned in American classrooms is representative of the dominant culture perspective, students need to know that this is the case, and to know that there are other cultural perspectives and interpretations that are also important to learn. In using the following example about time, students could be told, "In America speed and being on time are highly valued. People in other cultures may value taking more time to do things, and not give as much attention to being on time." When consciously explained in this manner, even the youngest students can begin to take on multiple cultural perspectives.

Students need to know why this lesson is worth learning, how it relates to their world, and can be applied to their lives. Culturally-transformative contextual teaching makes connections to the cultural background knowledge students already possess, integrates new learning with their background knowledge, and extends their learning for broader and deeper understanding of themselves and of the world's cultures.

As an example of establishing the context when the lesson question is, what is life like on Indian reservations today? To establish the context, the teacher can say "How many of you know what it is like to live on an Indian reservation today? Please raise your hands." Seek responses from the students who raised their hands and point out any misconceptions in student background knowledge. Then provide a brief accurate account of what life is like on Indian reservations today that would set the stage for what is to come in the lesson.

After developing the context, the culturally-transformative lesson is outlined and presented, both orally and through a written agenda to explain how the lesson will proceed. It is presented as outlined in the lesson agenda at the beginning of the lesson and used again as the lesson organizer during the lesson.

For example, in presenting the agenda the teacher can say, "This is our lesson in World/American cultures for today. The lesson objective or question that we will answer in the lesson is_____. First, I will _____. Second, we will work together to_____. Third, you will have an opportunity to show me what you have learned by_____."

When students know how the lesson will proceed at the outset, what they are accountable for doing during the lesson, and for demonstrating following the lesson, they are cued to what is expected of them. Teachers of effective culturally-transformative lessons present the agenda confidently and assertively so that students are motivated and engaged immediately as attentive interactive partners in their learning.

## Teaching the Lesson for Content Mastery and Ongoing Learning

Daily lessons are the smallest, the micro segment of content that teachers of culturally-transformative lessons set up for students to learn. Therefore, particular care is given to designing and teaching these lessons with a high level of precision and passion so that students learn them with few trials and that errors and confusion are minimized. The lesson agenda as (organizer) is the vehicle for conducting this form of careful precise teaching. It serves as the visible (agenda) for introducing the lesson at the beginning and as the (organizer) for keeping track of the lesson as it is taught. *At transition points, when the lesson proceeds from one phase or activity on the agenda to the next, it serves as the (anchor) for summarizing and stressing the critical attributes of what was learned in relationship to the overall lesson objective.*

The teachers' role during this first phase of teaching the culturally-transformative lesson, the information giving phase, is to use teaching strategies which help students understand in the clearest manner possible the concepts that are being taught. Teaching, therefore, emphasizes the **_structure and critical attributes_**, the points that define the essential qualities of the subject matter, and it gives special attention to important and difficult ideas.

During this phase of the lesson the content is structured and delivery proceeds at a relatively quick pace with many examples provided, many questions asked, and active participation encouraged. Recognizing that student learning styles, especially among culturally-diverse groups, are enhanced through the use of such strategies as demonstrations, oral narratives, visuals, manipulative materials, audio and visual aids, examples, diagrams, predictions, comparisons, and pattern identification these concrete materials and demonstrative approaches are employed in this phase of the lesson.

Effective teachers of culturally-transformative lessons recognize that, while it is important for students to figure out things for themselves, it is also helpful for them to see what productive behavior looks like. They help students learn a new behavior by having students watch them model the behavior and then try to imitate it. Through modeling, the visual modality is activated so that students not only hear how something is done they also see the behavior demonstrated. Clearly, modeling is very useful for non-dominant culture students. Teacher modeling of the behavior while the students observe and attend to the relevant elements of the modeling assists them in acquiring the behavior.

When continued learning is enhanced by the retention of previously learned skills and concepts such as multiplication facts, mph, or points on a globe, teaching focuses on helping students master the content and skills often to the point of over-learning. When this happens, students have a solid foundation (the rules and general knowledge) upon which to build later learning and they are able to use their developing knowledge and background for higher cognitive processing.

Students, who receive this quality of instruction during the information giving phase of culturally-transformative lessons, learn more and retain what they learn as the basis for future learning. This commitment and care is important for all students, and particularly for students from non-dominant cultures who may have little prior background in learning dominant-culture material.

Before moving to the next phase of the culturally-transformative lesson, teachers of culturally transformative lessons use the lesson agenda to summarize what was learned in this phase of the lesson in relation to the lesson objective. This action aids students in retaining the big ideas before moving on to the interactive phase of the lesson.

## Interacting with Students, Giving Them Directed Practice, and Encouraging Their Learning

Interacting with students in whole group culturally-transformative lessons occurs to a great degree through questioning which enables students to practice what they learned so far from phase one of the lesson with teacher assistance. The extent of teacher-assisted practice on concepts learned earlier in the content development phase of the lesson is a major determinant of student success. During this directed practice phase of the lesson, individualization within the group and the quality of learning elicited is dependent upon the kinds of questions asked, how the questions are asked, when the questions are asked, and to whom the questions are asked.

Equally important to the questioning process, is the quality of the interaction when responses to questions are elicited. In culturally-transformative lessons a range of questions are asked, timed and targeted to students in ways that enhance both students' learning and students' self-esteem. Teachers concentrate on asking easier questions to assure that all students have the greatest possible opportunity to become involved in the learning of the group. This asking of easier "recall-type questions" in combination with higher-level "why type questions" is what creates a dynamic within the group where all can contribute and learn from each other.

Accomplishing an interactive classroom dynamic is not easy. Questioning and responding to students during lessons are among the most challenging aspects of teaching, something that is never fully mastered. It requires both preparation and skill. The effort for teachers of culturally-transformative lessons begins by studying and knowing the content, designing levels of questions using a guide such as Bloom's Taxonomy (outlined at the end of this section), knowing the students, and carefully orchestrating the interaction and questioning of students during the act of teaching. The effort put forth in trying to accomplish this level and quality of student involvement is well worth it for this is truly the "heart of teaching."

*In culturally-transformative lessons student interaction can also occur in cooperative group or issue oriented dialog sessions as discussed earlier. These subgroups are formed during this phase of the lesson after students have obtained the necessary knowledge and preparation for these arrangements through the content development phase of the lesson.*

When students participate in these less-directive arrangements debriefing to assess the extent of participation and the extent of student learning is conducted in addition to other accountability mechanisms specific to the assigned task.

At the end of the interactive phase of the lesson, teachers of culturally-transformative lessons again use the lesson agenda to summarize, clarify, and focus on the learning objective before the lesson moves toward the accountability, independent practice phase of the lesson.

## Student Accountability, Independent Practice and Assessment

What students are accountable for learning in the lesson was to be explained to them up front as the lesson agenda was presented. Then special care was to be taken to ensure that what students were to be accountable for learning was taught in the first two phases of the lesson. During the first two phases of the lesson, information was provided by the teacher, followed by directed practice with the teacher through questioning and other forms of student-teacher, student-student interaction. Students in culturally-transformative lessons now have the opportunity and responsibility for demonstrating their understanding of what they learned in these two phases of the lesson. Student accountability may occur partially through an oral demonstration but, as an accountability mechanism, it also occurs independently through a written assessment.

In culturally-transformative lessons these quick assessments help teachers of effective culturally-transformative lessons determine where students are in relation to what was taught in this lesson and to the overall curriculum goals. Thorough teaching and attention to each student prior to and during the lesson usually results in a successful student demonstration of learning. The assessments help the teachers decide whether additional work is needed, and whether re-teaching, and remediation are necessary. Equally important, the assessments make it clear to students that each lesson is important to their learning, and it lets students know that they are accountable for being attentive, participating, and learning what is taught in each lesson.

In most instances, some form of additional practice is needed so that learning becomes firm (quick, accurate, and embedded in the student's schema). Teachers of effective culturally-transformative lessons make this decision based on the assessment and other factors. Frequent practice is particularly important in the early grades and with non-dominant culture students who may be coming in contact with the material for the first time. It may take a number of repetitions until students are firm in their understandings of content and quick and accurate in their skill development. At the beginning of new learning, practice periods are frequent and closely spaced. After the material is learned, practice continues but the amount of time between practices is extended. The foundation which these practice sessions can provide is important because it stimulates confidence and enables students to believe in their abilities.

For the most part, students are not able to apply their skill until they have attained mastery to the point of over learning or automaticity, or to apply their knowledge until they have learned the content in sufficient depth. For example, computation and problem solving in mathematics are facilitated when basic facts are learned to automaticity. There is also greater understanding and insight when students have learned a topic such as the reasons for the Civil War in depth and from multiple perspectives.

## Transfer, Discerning Relationships and Transferring Knowledge from One Context to Another

The most meaningful and useful phase of the lesson is transfer. Students' ability to see relationships and transfer information from one setting to another is what learning is all about. For students to develop this ability, it is necessary to consciously assist them in making connections between and among the abstract concepts and information typically learned in schools.

Even though it is impossible to teach everything, what is taught in culturally-transformative lessons is taught thoroughly so that students learn it fully. The ability to make use of knowledge in different contexts is a strong indicator of the extent to which it learned. It needs to be reiterated that students will be handicapped in their ability to transfer learning to new situations or give thoughtful opinions about it until they have a firm grasp of the knowledge and skills which are basic to such endeavors. In cultural transformative lessons essential skills and concepts are taught thoroughly to build a store of significant learning that students can use in multiple contexts to think critically and solve problems. The important question that each student is asked to answer is how does this information relate to my life, how does it apply in the real world?

Benjamin Bloom's well-known classification system is used to develop learning arrangements which enable students to extend, apply, and transfer information. Greatly simplified, the levels of Bloom's taxonomy are:

<u>Knowledge</u>. At this level students obtain information to use for more complex thinking. These facts are essential to higher levels of thinking.

<u>Comprehension or Understanding</u>. This level of thinking requires that students understand the information they are learning and not merely recall or parrot information. Having students explain in their own words is helpful to understanding.

These first two levels of thinking, the possession of information and understanding that information establish the foundation upon which complex thinking is built.

<u>Application</u>. At this level students apply what they have learned to new situations. This ability to transfer knowledge is a very important goal in learning since we cannot nor should we teach everything.

<u>Analysis</u>. This level requires that students take a part or categorize information, seeing similarity in different things and differences in similar things, thus reducing complexity in their world.

<u>Synthesis</u>. This level requires the bringing together of more than one piece of information, idea, concept, or set of skills and the creation of new categories to organize the information such as creating a model, developing a hypothesis, or writing an original story.

<u>Evaluation or Judgment</u>. This is the highest level of thinking in the taxonomy. When making an evaluation or judgment, there is no right or wrong answer until the evidence

used to support that answer or conclusion is considered. It calls for teachers to ask students to support their opinions or judgments with data. Without such evidence, asking students to give their opinions tends to result in haphazard guessing.

It is not critical that teachers be able to identify or label the precise level of Bloom's Taxonomy, though it is important to understand the complexity of thought required at each level. The essential idea is first to help students develop a store of information which they understand and then to stimulate students to think beyond simply recalling that information.

Part One of this volume has been devoted to explaining the effective teaching of culturally-transformative lessons to build cross-cultural understanding and excellence in student learning. The phases of teaching illustrated how the research and evidence-based competencies combine in the context of preparing for and teaching culturally-transformative lessons. Most of us long to be able to address the diverse learning needs of students in our classrooms by being as proficient with these teaching competencies as described in this section. Some of us may believe that our teaching is already at this level, but how to be sure? Just having the competencies and their application in lessons, gives us a general idea of how we think we are teaching; however, when we have only a perception amid the teaching variables, it is difficult to pinpoint specifically what we are doing while teaching. To really analyze and develop our skill in teaching, it is necessary to segregate the competencies into distinct behaviors so that we can consciously focus on each behavior one at a time as we employ them in our lessons.

Part Two, the next section of this volume, isolates the competencies into discrete behaviors. Then, Part Three sets up a process that we can use to continuously grow in the process of teaching culturally-transformative lessons.

## Positive Behavior

## Positive Climate

## Establishing Set

## Optimizing Time

## Clarity

_____ ?

1. _____

## Assessing/ Monitoring Progress

2. _____

## Using Questions

3. _____

## Feedback/ Reinforcement

4. _____

## Developing Thinking/Ability

## Transfer

# Part Two: The Culturally-Transformative Teaching Model

Part Two presents and explains the Culturally-Transformative Teaching Model with its components: the teaching principles, performance indicators, lesson framework, and lesson agenda for you to use as a template to grow systematically in teaching culturally-transformative lessons. After the presentation and explanation of these components, a beginning teacher shows how the components come together in a culturally-transformative lesson. Her modeling is sure to be reassuring; it instills confidence and a belief that every teacher has the talent and ability to learn and grow continuously in the complex act of culturally-transformative teaching whether the teacher is just beginning or has been teaching for a while. The teaching of culturally-transformative lessons, as the model shows, is a comprehensive dynamic process. When you implement the model systematically and thoroughly as described, you are en route to becoming a thoughtful discerning master teacher who is committed to building cross-cultural understanding and assuring excellence in student learning.

## The Components of the Culturally-Transformative Teaching Model

The Culturally-Transformative Teaching Model as depicted in this section is designed help you develop the teaching competencies outlined in Part One of this volume. The teaching principles and performance indicators set forth in the model are the competencies for teaching effective culturally transformative lessons isolated as teaching behaviors. The function of the model is to help you learn to *consciously* attend to and employ these behaviors in your lessons as you teach. Others can also observe and give you feedback on your growth and effectiveness in employing the principles and performance indicators in your lessons. Effectiveness in teaching culturally-transformative lessons calls for you to learn and practice employing the behaviors in your lessons progressively and routinely on a daily basis. Their use will become part of your teaching repertoire through systematic concentration and practice as you build your expertise over time. As you will see in Part Three, the model can also be set up to develop the expertise of groups of teachers in the school-as-a-whole.

The Culturally-Transformative Teaching Model that is presented in this section has been a long-lasting passion that brings together years of thought and involvement with others in several school districts, public and private schools, and at the university level designing systems to improve teaching. Those who have used the model to develop their teaching skill are thrilled with it and find that it works.

The teaching competencies, discussed in Part One of this volume, came about as part of a consultant project. The involvement with the school faculty, as part of this project, led to a supervision and evaluation process based on the competencies. The teachers welcomed the process, they became familiar with the research as well, and they found the competencies and process to be credible and workable in a range of classrooms and grade levels (K-12) for all subject matter including art and physical education. At this point we only had the competencies noted and applied intuitively by each teacher and stated generally as criteria on the teacher evaluation form. There was no formalized process for teachers to develop the teaching behaviors that would lead them to demonstrate the competencies during the act of teaching.

Later, at the university, we formalized the process and created a teaching model for teacher candidates in the School of Education. Our concern was not just to evaluate the teaching of our students but to develop their teaching skill and the skill of their mentor teachers in the schools as well. Both needed to learn and to demonstrate the behaviors necessary to plan and teach effective culturally-transformative lessons. The students needed to learn and demonstrate the behaviors in their teaching and the mentor teachers needed to learn and model the behaviors for the students. In the process of identifying the principles and performance indicators as components to be included in the teaching model, there were numerous deliberations with colleagues, mentor teachers, and others about the process.

The question was what are the qualities that are most applicable to teaching a lesson to build cross-cultural understanding and promote excellence in student learning? And, how can we put the qualities in a succinct format so that the prospective teachers and their mentors/supervisors can learn them and document their use in the context of a series of lessons over the course of a semester? We pondered these questions over time and after some discussion about ways to operationalize the competencies from Part One decided on the following components:

- The Ten Teaching Principles
- The Ten Performance Indicators
- The Lesson Framework
- The Lesson Agenda

Together these components, along with guidelines and procedures, make up the Culturally-Transformative Teaching Model. After considering each of the components separately, you have an opportunity to see how they interrelate and come together in a dynamic lesson. A teacher, in the introductory stages of learning and employing the components in her teaching, provides insights into her thinking as she plans for and engages in teaching a culturally-transformative lesson.

# The Teaching Principles and Performance Indicators, the Substance of Culturally Transformative Lessons

## The Ten Teaching Principles

The ten teaching principles which comprise the culturally-transformative teaching model are the qualities which are consistently identified in the research, as expressed earlier in Part One, as being correlated with student learning. They are the essence of teaching which you can use to guide and give structure to your teaching in academic and other dimensions of classroom practice. Careful and consistent application of these principles in lessons enables you to achieve excellence in student learning and build cross-cultural understanding. The ten principles and the other components of culturally-transformative teaching can help you develop, and assess your skill in teaching and lesson management. They are:

1. Establishing Set/ Context for the Lesson
2. Making Optimum Use of Time during the Lesson
3. Facilitating a Positive Climate
4. Maintaining Positive Behavior
5. Providing Clarity in Teaching
6. Asking Questions, Responding to, and Supporting Students During the Lesson
7. Assessing and Monitoring Student Progress during the Lesson
8. Providing Feedback/ Reinforcement during the Lesson
9. Developing Student Thinking and Ability during the Lesson (Metacognition)
10. Promoting Transfer of Learning during the Lesson

## The Ten Teaching Principles and Their Performance Indicators

The ten teaching principles in combination with their performance indicators are explained and analyzed below. The performance indicators are the teaching effectiveness, cognitive learning, and evidence-based competencies which define and give substance to the teaching principles-in-action and serve to guide and structure the teaching and lesson management process. They give specificity in knowing what to do and how to do it when applying each of the teaching principles. In some instances, the principles and indicators are the recommended applications of classroom practices that have been developed in other volumes, most notably Volume II, *Improving Classroom Practice through Culturally-Inclusive Classroom Management.*

The identified indicators are not all-inclusive. There is purposeful overlap between and among the performance indicators and some may apply to more than one teaching principle. Overall, however, the principles and indicators, in combination, provide a balanced arrangement of research and evidence-based teaching practice. They make teaching predictable, enabling teachers and others to know what comprises effective culturally-transformative teaching, and they provide a clearly defined systematic way to examine and improve teaching. Of the outlined principles and indicators, those associated with establishing set and transfer, for introducing and concluding lessons, are the most relevant and important for transforming dominant-culture material.

In this professional development series teaching is decision making. Consequently, while all teaching principles should be considered for application in a lesson, it is for you to decide when, how, and whether a performance indicator is applicable in a given teaching situation. Equally important, in the decision-making process is for you to be able to explain why a performance indicator is or is not applicable. The teaching principles and their performance indicators are depicted in the section which follows:

**Principle 1. Establishing Set/Context for the Lesson**

Establishing set is crucial to teaching, lesson management and to building cross-cultural understanding. The following ten performance indicators of establishing set show what to do to demonstrate this principle and ensure that students have the readiness and requisite background to engage, participate, and learn during the lesson:

- Provide a cultural orientation for the material (Western, American, Non-western, etc.)
- Introduce the lesson through material that is broader in scope than the lesson (world-wide--U.S. context)
- Provide a rationale and purpose for the lesson.
- Use a novel approach to capture student attention.
- Determine what students already know about the material and explain how the lesson will add to their knowledge, skill, and future learning.
- Show how the new material relates to previously studied material, the broader curriculum, and to real-world experiences.
- Establish procedures for interacting during the lesson: expectations for participating and learning, readiness and use of materials, behavior and attitudes, etc.
- Use an outline (lesson agenda) to communicate the lesson's objective (the lesson question) and to give the sequence (the order) in which the lesson will be taught.
- Show enthusiasm for the material giving assurances and expectations for the success of all students.
- Establish student accountability for learning by pointing out what students will do to demonstrate their learning during and at the end of the lesson.

As you can see from the performance indicators, the principle of establishing set, the context for the lesson—is crucial. This principle calls for you to *set up your lessons to ensure student success.* If you set up your lesson well, your likelihood of success is magnified. On the other hand, if you fail to fully set up your lesson and exclude applicable performance indicators, the success of your lesson may be diminished. It is important to note that in establishing set, the context should be precise, to the point, and accomplished in 3-5 minutes.

**Principle 2. Making Optimum Use of Time During the Lesson**

Making effective use of time is important in all phases of the lesson. The performance indicators below were fully developed in Volume II, the classroom management volume of the series. Here they state specifically how to demonstrate this principle and make optimum use of time in the lesson:

- Assure that students know and follow classroom routines.
- Use a lesson agenda (sequence of activities) to set expectations, pace the lesson flow, facilitate transitions, and keep students engaged and on-task.
- Provide clear directions and assure student understanding and follow-through when initiating activities within the lesson.
- Arrange for materials use and efficient procedures in advance of the lesson.
- Maintain momentum, a smooth relatively rapid lesson pace without disruptions, digressions, and "down time."
- Manage transitions, conceptual shifts or changes in procedure, so that activity flows smoothly.
- Alert students in advance to changes in emphasis, topic, or procedure.
- Employ transition activities between lessons.
- Display an ability for "overlapping," doing more than one thing at a time.
- Give attention to and structure student movement during changes in the instructional setting.

The indicators involved in optimizing time are very important to achieving your classroom goals. Managing time in the classroom tends to be challenging for beginning teachers. The agenda helps you and your students manage time during the lesson. You can post and use the agenda so that both you and your students are able to keep pace and remain conscious of operating within the allotted time frame.

**Principle 3. Facilitating a Positive Climate During the Lesson**

The following performance indicators help you create an instructional climate which promotes cross-cultural understanding and facilitates learning. They state what to do to demonstrate skill in applying this principle:

- Structure activities to assure student success and positive interactions.
- Encourage an atmosphere in which students feel free to take risks and make mistakes.

- Provide an instructional setting which promotes eye contact and encourages students to be attentive.
- Serve as a model for students to emulate (voice quality, movement, smiles and warmth).
- Display a calm, firm, caring, consistent manner.
- Praise appropriate behavior through such phrases as " I like the way…" and "Thank you for…" while deemphasizing misbehavior, ("catch 'em being good").
- Use praise to shape behavior in the desired direction.
- Promote caring equitable learning opportunities through participation, support, etc.
- Recognize and develop student's multiple intelligences, building on their strengths.
- Model empathy and sensitivity toward others by creating a community of learners who empathize with and support each other.

The indicators associated with positive climate are what you do to provide an atmosphere in which students from all cultural groups can feel supported and included in the learning process. Your smiles, warmth, calm, firm, caring and consistent demeanor in an environment that encourages risk taking will go a long way to helping all students feel respected and supported.

**Principle 4. Maintaining Positive Behavior**

Developing and maintaining positive student behavior is important and often the biggest classroom management challenge especially if you are a beginning teacher. The following performance indicators state what you do to demonstrate skill in applying this principle:

- Provide clear and consistent expectations for student behavior at the beginning of the lesson.
- Give emphasis to positively reinforcing appropriate behavior.
- Stimulate attention and take appropriate action before a problem arises.
- Meet challenges to your behavior expectations until expectations and procedures become the norm.
- Use non-verbal approaches—proximity, eye contact, facial expression, gestures, and vocal variation to manage behavior.
- Display "withitness," awareness of what's going on in class at all times.
- Follow through with accelerating (less assertive to more assertive) teacher behavior to obtain compliance with rules.
- Respond to infractions immediately, firmly, and without harsh action.
- Employ logical consequences and helping students see a link between their actions and the consequence.
- Preserve student dignity—no public reprimands, sarcasm, humiliation.

While all principles apply to maintaining positive behavior, those that relate to being proactive by setting behavior expectations up front, positively reinforcing appropriate behavior, and taking action before a problem arises should be given clear attention. They call for you to teach directly how you want students to behave.

**Principle 5. Clarity in Instruction During the Lesson**

Clarity in teaching needs to be planned and given careful attention before and during the lesson. The following performance indicators are goals of this professional development series and should aid clear and concise communication in lessons. They state what you do to demonstrate skill in applying this principle:

- Focus the lesson so that the structure (key ideas) of the discipline and its critical attributes are emphasized throughout the lesson.
- State (lead students to) the objective of the lesson (answering the lesson question).
- Present and use an agenda to structure and teach the lesson sequentially, to summarize, build connections among points in learning, alert students to upcoming events, etc.
- Give explicit step-by-step directions as needed at transition points during the lesson.
- Ask students questions to monitor their understanding of what has been taught.
- Re teach parts of the lesson as needed before moving on.
- Have students summarize the main points of the lesson in their own words at transition points and at the end of the lesson.
- Speak and project words clearly, varying dynamics, pace, and intonation within a range that is conducive to understanding.
- Use concrete and varied examples, visuals, models, and demonstrations to aid understanding for all cultures.
- Give detailed and redundant explanations for difficult points.

The use of a lesson agenda/organizer as the primary visual for the lesson is very likely the single most facilitating device for assuring clarity in your teaching. Most of the designated performance indicators for clarity can be demonstrated through the use of a lesson agenda. It is important to note that clarity in speech and the use of visuals and examples are essential for ensuring understanding and for teaching students from non-dominant cultures.

**Principle 6. Using Questions: Asking Questions During the Lesson**

The interactive process of asking questions and responding to students following questioning are among the most challenging principles in teaching but crucial to the learning process. Practice on the following performance indicators helps you develop questioning skill and demonstrate skill in applying this principle:

- Use an initiating question to present the lesson objective to focus student learning during the lesson.
- Ask prior questions to guide and foster learning from an experience (field trips, videos, the teacher read-aloud, etc.) Support students' listening/observation abilities by setting up the task, for example, "I want you to listen/watch for these three (3) things…"
- Use questions for different purposes within the lesson:
  -To focus learning in a particular direction
  -To increase student engagement
  -To guide students through learning tasks
  -To monitor understanding
- Use questioning patterns which encourage maximum student participation:
  -non volunteers
  -ordered turns
  -unison responses
  -signals, mini chalkboards, manipulative materials
- Use multiple level questions from Bloom's Taxonomy to engage, individualize, and challenge students.
- Use both convergent questions and divergent questions, and encourage student initiated questions.
- Use open-ended questions to encourage multiple answers/solutions/perspectives within the group.
- Use a large number of "easy" questions and equal distribution of questions to increase student motivation, involvement, and achievement.
- Use fast-paced questions to promote automaticity in skill development.
- Direct questions to the group—then, before calling on a student use "wait time" (3-5 seconds) to promote depth in student thinking.

There are multiple reasons for asking questions and multiple ways to ask questions. The performance indicators illustrate some of the most important and useful ways. Asking questions and responding to students during questioning are areas which you can and very likely will pursue over the course of your career. Use questions to enhance student participation, to promote automaticity in skill development, and to promote depth in thinking and processing information.

**Using Questions: Responding to and Supporting Students during Questioning**

After asking a question, the challenge is to respond to students in a way that encourages their continued participation. The following performance indicators help you meet this challenge and demonstrate skill in applying this principle:

- Ask students to think and prepare before responding.
- Provide opportunities for students to share with others before responding.
- Avoid such nonspecific overworked expressions as "good job."
- Handle incorrect student responses by:
  - Rephrasing questions at lower levels of thinking
  - Supplying additional information
  - Giving clues to the answer/solution
  - Re-teaching
  - Giving the appropriate response when other efforts fail.
- Dignify each student's response by staying with the student—and by refraining from referring the question to another student.
- Encourage thorough and multiple perspectives/solutions to open-ended questions.
- Reinforce a response by relating it to points in the learning.
- Support students, acknowledging partial answers while encouraging more complete answers by:
  - Prompting-encouraging students to expand their answers, give examples, evidence to support answers.
  - Probing- asking for more specificity, rationale, and reasoning behind a response.
  - Perspective taking-having several students respond to the same question from different points of view.
- Build student self-concept through positive reinforcement by asking the "right" question to the "right" student at the "right" time.

In contrast to the typical approach to calling on a student and moving on, or calling on someone else when the student responds incorrectly, the performance indicators provide a range of responses that you can use. The ideal remains. You need to know your students well enough to ask the right question to the right student, making it likely that the student will respond correctly so that you can give positive feedback and build the student's self-esteem in the process.

**Principle 7. Assessing and Monitoring Student Progress During the Lesson**

Assessing and monitoring progress during teaching is a dynamic approach to stimulating student learning in-process. It calls for alertness and checking for student understanding before moving on in the teaching sequence. Use of the following performance indicators demonstrates your skill in applying this principle:

- Prepare students to do well by alerting them to their accountability prior to teaching the lesson.
- Assess to determine and build student background knowledge prior to beginning the lesson.
- Use close and careful monitoring during the early stages of learning to build students' store of background knowledge.

- Assess and monitor student progress at transition points during the lesson to check for understanding before proceeding to the next phase of the lesson.
- Actively monitor and check on students who are likely to have difficulty during the lesson; ensure that <u>all</u> students learn relevant skills and concepts.
- Provide for quick assessment during the lesson by using such strategies and concrete materials as mini chalkboards, signals, and other manipulative materials.
- Give students strategies for monitoring their own progress.
- Debrief at the end of the lesson by having students state/demonstrate the extent of their learning, what they have learned, and why it's important.
- Assess and monitor student progress through a written assessment following your teaching to determine the extent of student learning and your teaching effectiveness.
- Examine and give students feedback on their written assessments.

These performance indicators, when combined with thorough precise teaching, keep students from "falling through the cracks." In this way your teaching is thorough and student learning is greatly enhanced.

## Principle 8. Providing Feedback/Reinforcement During the Lesson

Keeping students informed about their performance during the lesson and helping them to feel positive and encouraged about their participation is important to teacher-student interaction. Use of the following performance indicators demonstrates skill in applying this principle:

- Provide specific, immediate feedback to inform students about the accuracy and quality of their performance, indicating what they can do to improve.
- Use praise to express appreciation for student effort and/or accomplishment. Specify what is being praised.
- Use praise early in the learning process to increase student motivation.
- Give close attention and support to struggling students with lots of positive reinforcement, particularly with new learning.
- Avoid ambiguous overworked phrases such as "you were good today," "good job," "wow," or "great." Use a variety of phrases to give reinforcement to students.
- Provide a variety of opportunities for students to perform and receive feedback on their performances.
- Create opportunities for students to gauge their own performance.
- Use a variety of forms of positive reinforcement—nods, smiles, proximity, etc.
- Back verbal praise with non-verbal approval.
- Use public praise with young students; praise older students privately.

The use of feedback helps students to assess their own performance; praise provides the positive dimension that supports and keeps students in all cultural groups engaged and striving to do even better. Your use of praise to express appreciation to students can be very beneficial and enhancing.

**Principle 9. Developing Student Thinking and Ability During the Lesson (Metacognition)**

With this principle students think about what they are learning, why they are learning it, and how they are learning it. Application of the following performance indicators demonstrates your skill in applying this principle:

- Convey high expectations for all students in the quality of praise, content, acceptance, participation, encouragement.
- Activate and build student background knowledge prior to lessons.
- Encourage multiple perspectives on dominant-culture material.
- Promote higher level thinking about material through analysis, synthesis, and evaluation of concepts/questions.
- Accommodate the 3 sensory channels through visual, auditory, kinesthetic devices.
- Accommodate field dependent/independent cognitive styles—right and left brain modalities, holistic and step-by-step thinking.
- Promote in-depth thinking and multiple perspectives through probing questions and challenges to learning concepts.
- Provide motivating tasks with moderate tension to challenge and elevate student ability levels.
- Use technology, other media, and strategies to accommodate different learning styles and preferences.
- Use metacognitive approaches to help students learn how to think, to reason, to learn.

The performance indicators encourage students to engage in critical pedagogy through higher levels of Bloom's taxonomy, in-depth thinking, and metacognitive approaches. When you activate and build on student background knowledge you can promote excellence in learning and build cultural understanding through your lessons.

**Principle 10. Promoting Transfer of Learning During the Lesson**

The principle of transfer connects with establishing set, in reestablishing the context, the significance of the lesson and its relevance in student's lives. It recognizes that when students learn skills and concepts well and are able to see connections, they begin to have the flexibility to extend and apply what they are learning in multiple contexts. They have the background to question circumstances and pursue resolutions. The following performance indicators demonstrate skill in applying this principle:

- Teach essential skills for mastery, and concepts for depth in understanding and application
- Emphasize relevance and understanding—how the lesson relates to and has "real world" applications.
- Explain how the lesson relates to the overall curriculum goals.
- Conclude lessons by having students state what they learned, why it is important, how it can be applied in "real world" settings.
- Show how the new learning adds to what students already knew and will aid future learning.
- Teach transferrable learning skills for future applications (reading strategies, sequencing, problem solving strategies, etc.
- Emphasize process over content—learning how to learn and to analyze content for cross-cultural relevance.
- Help students make connections and see relationships in what they are learning.
- Teach to and build on student strengths.
- Build global knowledge for understanding by teaching content from the view point of multiple cultures and from multiple perspectives.

Relevance and real-world applications, building students' store of knowledge, global understanding, and teaching content from the view point of multiple cultures and multiple perspectives, places this principle and performance indicators at the forefront in terms of developing students' cross-cultural understanding. Your teaching should have the ultimate goal of transfer for real-world applications.

Now that you have an overview of the 10 teaching principles and performance indicators, you have a basic understanding of how the teaching competencies have been isolated into teaching behaviors that can be learned and observed. These behaviors are delineated in a linear fashion and this is a useful way to learn them for this format enables you to pinpoint and practice them until they become a part of your teaching repertoire. Teaching, however, is a complex coordinated process that is more than the sum of its parts. In an actual lesson the teaching principles and their indicators are interwoven to create a smooth integrated performance. The lesson framework and lesson agenda are the organizers that enable this smooth integrated performance.

## The Lesson Framework and Lesson Agenda, the Organizers of Culturally-Transformative Lessons

The lesson framework is particularly unique and noteworthy for its sensitivity to multiple cultures. It captures the field-dependent and right hemisphere cognitive styles of cultures that tend to benefit from more holistic situations that are imbedded in social context. Similarly, it captures the field independent and left hemisphere cognitive styles of cultures that tend to stress facts, detail, and linear step-by-step teaching. It calls for you, at the outset of each lesson, to place the curriculum content into a broader context and apprise students of the cultural orientation and differing cultural perspectives surrounding the content. Through its contextual ***whole-part-whole*** format, wherein you begin the lesson with (the whole) the context, teach (the parts) sequentially, and conclude the lesson by reestablishing (the whole) the context, you embrace both field dependent and field independent styles of learning. The lesson framework provides the basic structure for the design and implementation of culturally-transformative lessons.

The Lesson Framework for Culturally-Transformative Teaching is depicted on page 53. This framework for teaching lessons provides the basic structure upon which to develop and refine your skill in teaching. It helps you teach sequentially and systematically and can serve as a checklist for you or a mentor to use to guide your teaching. The Lesson Framework calls for you to employ the five (5) episodes as they appear in the framework in the following manner:

___Provide a context (introduction) for the lesson:
___Gain attention through novelty; material broader in scope than the lesson
___Activate background knowledge.
___Give the rationale and purpose for the lesson.
___Connect the lesson to common "real world" experiences; other cultural orientations
___Show how the lesson content relates to the broader curriculum, previous learning, and will add to future learning.

___Begin the lesson:
___Set expectations for using materials, participating, behaving, and overall accountability.
___Present the lesson agenda: The lesson question/objective and the sequence of activities.

___Teach according to the lesson agenda:
___Build toward answering the lesson question. Example:
    (1) teacher input,
    (2) interactive processing and scaffolding, and
    (3) student accountability.

___Manage the Lesson by using transition points to:
- Summarize and make connections among points in learning.
- Assess and monitor student understanding.
- Give feedback and praise to students.
- Alert and structure changes in emphasis, topic, procedure, movement
- Provide directions for the next activity.
- Stimulate attention and reinforce expectations
- Assess student thinking and learning, and adjust teaching approach
- Debrief to assure that students can answer the lesson question.

___Reestablish the context (conclusion) for the lesson:
___Have students share what they learned, why it is important, and how it relates to/can be applied in other situations.
___Show how the new learning adds to what students already knew and will add to future learning.

# The Lesson Agenda

The lesson agenda is the part of the lesson framework that is to be placed on the instructional board or chart paper, explained, and used to structure and implement the lesson with your students.

**Note that the lesson agenda is episode three of the lesson framework.** All five episodes of the lesson framework should be followed as you plan for and teach your lesson.

The structure of the lesson agenda is depicted below:
The lesson question/ the major objective stated as a question?
(1) teacher input,
(2) interactive processing and scaffolding
(3) independent assessment for student accountability.

The lesson Agenda will be explained in greater detail later in this volume along with other lesson management tools. Essentially, though, the agenda is a simplified structure (outline/organizer/anchor/agenda) for the lesson, which you display visually on the instructional board or chart, and at the same time explain orally to students. Its strength is that it allows students to both *see and hear* your explanation of the lesson as-a-whole before dealing with the parts.

Virtuosity, in the sense of being able to compose and perform a piece with beginning, middle, and end—theme, variation, repetition, rhythm, emphasis and continuity—is within your grasp if you employ the whole-part-whole lesson framework. Your lessons can be powerful in terms of student learning and, when delivered with skill and finesse through the use of the lesson agenda, the lesson can flow like a symphonic piece. Aside from the beauty and style which you can exhibit, culturally transformative pedagogy addresses the major premise of this book—to give students the information and skill they need to transform what they typically learn in dominant-culture classrooms, and broaden their perspectives to promote cross-cultural understanding. By adhering to the processes outlined in the lesson framework, it is possible for you to be thorough, precise, and productive in teaching your lessons.

# A Model Culturally-Transformative Lesson: Using the Lesson Framework to Integrate the Teaching Principles, and Performance Indicators in the Lesson

In the description below you will be able to see, through the eyes of a beginning teacher, how the ten teaching principles and their performance indicators can come together in a lesson through the Lesson Framework for Culturally Transformative Teaching and how your facility with the lesson agenda makes it all possible. **The diagrams and highlighted portions show where each of the 10 principles fits into the lesson framework.** The description helps you see how the process works, and how you can consider and apply the teaching principles and performance indicators in your teaching.

---

## A Teacher Learns to Use the Ten Teaching Principles in a Lesson

Good lessons help students learn. And to have good lessons takes time, effort, and skill. My teaching skill will develop over time as I make the effort to learn and incorporate the ten teaching principles into my teaching style. The ten teaching principles are establishing set, optimizing instructional time, using questions, providing clear instruction, monitoring students' progress, providing feedback and reinforcement, creating a positive climate, maintaining positive behavior, promoting transfer of learning, and developing student thinking. **The Organizing Framework for Teaching a Lesson provides the structure for designing and teaching lessons that incorporate the Ten Teaching Principles. This Framework calls for outlining and delivering lessons to students through The Lesson Agenda. Ways to incorporate each of the Ten Principles of Teaching**

**through the Framework and Agenda will be emphasized as each principle is explained.** It will take time and practice, but once I learn how to use the lesson framework, lesson agenda, and all ten principles appropriately, I will be able to provide my students with great lessons—introduced with flair and delivered with precision—to increase their learning.

**Setting Up and Establishing the Context for the Lesson (Principle 1)**

The first teaching principle that I must learn to use in my lessons is establishing the context—setting up and outlining the lesson in a way that provides instant clarity, what the lesson is about, where the lesson is going, and how we can work together to get there. In establishing the context, I am concerned with developing the context (Big Picture) surrounding my teaching segment, how it relates to the broader curriculum and the "real world" including the diverse and multicultural perspectives associated with the concepts to be presented. I must capture students, attention and use novel approaches to make my lesson come alive. Students need to know why they should learn certain material, and I need to find out how much they know so that I can build a bridge from what they already know to what they will be learning. Setting expectations for using materials, for participating and behaving during the lesson, and the students' accountability for learning are all essential parts of setting up the lesson. **At the outset of every lesson, I will seek to motivate, set the context and expectations for learning, and lead my students to the Lesson Agenda which I will have written on the board. During this introductory phase of my lesson, I will present the Agenda orally to students by explaining how the lesson will proceed and how we will work and learn together during the lesson.** To be an effective skilled teacher, I must gain my students' attention, interest, and engagement by setting up the lesson at the beginning before I teach it.

**Optimizing Time (Principle 2)**

Research has shown that students who spend more time in teacher-directed academic activities learn more; therefore, the second teaching principle that I will learn to use in my lessons is optimizing time. I must begin on time, keep my lessons moving, and end on time. Through optimization of instructional time, maintaining momentum, and making smooth transitions, I will be able to spend more time on task and increase student learning. In addition to achieving smooth transitions between lessons, I must also be conscious of transitions between activities within the lesson, and of giving clear directions for procedures both at the beginning and at transition points during the lesson. Maintaining momentum within my lessons is very important. I will teach at a relatively brisk pace with great enthusiasm for what I am teaching. Then, by making eye contact and slowing down at transition points between activities to

assure that my students are with me, I can develop a rhythm and timing that is appropriate for me and my students, while also gauging my ability to stay within the allotted time frame. Time is precious and in order to get through everything, I must be organized, avoid jerkiness and digressions, and maintain conceptual flow. **The most important part of optimizing time is to know what I am teaching and have the key points stated in a written Agenda. Then, by using my Lesson Agenda at transition points to take stock of my timing, I will be able to keep things organized and flowing smoothly.**

## Creating a Positive Climate (Principle 3)

The third teaching principle that I will learn to use in my lessons is to create a positive climate. Teaching in an encouraging atmosphere is important to students' learning. As a teacher I need to make sure my students know that I appreciate and care for all of them. I must be a positive role model for my students and encourage positive interaction between them. If I want to increase learning, I must make all my students feel valued, cared for, and supported. Students should be able to answer questions and participate in class without being embarrassed or criticized if they make a mistake. I must try my best to have good student-teacher eye contact. This will make the students feel important and encourage them to pay attention. **By slowing down at transition points in the lesson, making eye contact and giving as much attention to "how my students are doing" as I do to the "stuff" I'm teaching, I am doing my best to provide my students with a positive climate and therefore enhance their learning experience**.

## Maintaining Positive Behavior (Principle 4)

Maintaining student attention and engagement during my lessons is likely to present many challenges for me. This brings me to the fourth teaching principle. As a teacher I will have to be positive with my students in order to make sure that my students maintain positive behavior. Teachers are role models to their students and if they do not have a positive approach with their students, they cannot count on the students to have one either. **When I set up my lessons, I will inform my students of my expectations for participation and behaving during my lessons. Also, to monitor activity, maintain student interest, and take corrective action without disrupting learning, I will use my Lesson Agenda at transition points during the lesson to stimulate attention and reinforce appropriate behavior.** In order to maintain positive behavior, I must be consistent in enforcing my expectations and in taking action before problems arise. Non-verbal approaches and positive reinforcement are the best ways to try to address the situation. If it is necessary for me to respond to student misbehavior, I must remember to preserve students' dignity and avoid confrontations. I know it is going to be hard for me to focus on teaching good lessons and on making sure that all students maintain positive behavior, but I know I must learn to accomplish both. Effective teaching and learning can only occur when I have positive expectations, consistency, and mutual respect.

## Instructional Clarity (Principle 5)

I think the most important aspect of teaching is providing instructional clarity. This refers to the teacher's ability to provide instruction that helps students come to a clear understanding of the material being presented. The fifth teaching principle that I will concentrate on in my lessons is to be clear in my teaching. Nothing is worse than being told to do something, without having a clear understanding of how to do it. Students are the same way and I need to remember that as I teach my lesson. I must speak clearly, give thorough step-by-step directions, and insure that everyone listens, understands, and can repeat the directions. I must organize my lesson content and activities in a logical manner that students will find obvious. The lesson content must have clear objectives and the ability to be presented in a step-by-step manner. I must emphasize important points in my lesson by repeating them, pausing, and then reviewing them again. I must of course have clear focused instruction throughout, and make sure that everyone understands at each step before going on. At the end of the lesson, it is very important that I summarize the major points once again for my students. **By presenting and using the Lesson Agenda, I have a guide before me to keep me on task and to assure that all students are with me, and by referring to it at transition points during the lesson, students know what is going on as I move from one activity to the next.** This will insure clear precise teaching which offers every student an equal opportunity to learn.

## Using Questions and Responding to Students (Principle 6)

About one-third of classroom interactions happen in the form of question-answer sessions between teacher and student. And, students tend to learn more when they are actively engaged in the question and answer session. The sixth teaching principle that I will learn to use in my lessons is asking questions and responding to students in ways that support and encourage their participation. **By beginning each lesson with the focusing question contained in my Lesson Agenda, students immediately know what the overall lesson aims to accomplish.** Asking questions to my students is a good way to get them to think. For example, I will also have an opportunity to engage students and move them toward higher levels of understanding through questions based on Bloom's taxonomy. By questioning my students, I can move learning in a particular direction, help students connect what they are learning to their current knowledge base, and help students understand how what they are learning applies to their everyday lives. During a lesson if I feel that a few students are not getting the information, or if they seem lost, I can ask questions to get them back on track and keep their attention. I will seek ways to give all students a chance to participate and become involved in the lesson. I will use questions for different purposes—open-ended questions followed by "wait time" (3-5 seconds) when I want to promote depth in thinking, as well as "rapid fire" questions when I want to develop automaticity in skill development.

By asking questions and responding to the answers students give, I give the students a good idea of areas where they need to focus and areas where they are doing well. I also have to remember that, particularly in culturally-diverse classrooms a number of answers could be correct. Not all students are going to answer the same question in the same way. I will allow more than one student to answer a question so that I can get multiple responses. Hopefully this will make all students want to get involved. The sensitivity that I use in responding to students answers will be very important to building their self-esteem during questioning. As a basic rule, I will stay with a student and give hints, clues, and re-teaching. When an appropriate response is not forthcoming, I will give students the answer and move on. I will avoid the commonly used practice of calling on another student to help a struggling student, for this only serves to reinforce the student's view of her or his inability. Above all, when a student takes the risk of venturing a response during questioning, I will find a way to dignify the student's response. I will encourage all students to ask questions whenever they need to. Using questions is a good way to promote student/teacher interaction. **<u>Using assessment questions during transition points in the lesson can show me whether students get he "hang of things" or whether students still need more work. I can then decide whether to re teach or move on with the next phase of the lesson.</u>**

1.____
2.____
3.____

## Developing Student Thinking and Ability-Meta-Cognition (Principle 7)

The seventh teaching principle that I will learn to use in my lessons is developing students thinking and ability. If I wish to develop my students' ability levels, I must teach them how to think. To do this, I must be aware of my students' background knowledge, set high expectations for all students, and provide a positive classroom climate that values different ideas and points of view. Meta-cognition, thinking and talking about thinking as it occurs in the classroom, is a great way to develop students' abilities. Meta-cognition requires students to monitor, reflect upon, and improve their learning strategies and problem solving. I must do as much as possible to help increase my student's meta-cognitive abilities, this will help them learn to summarize to increase reading comprehension or to adjust their reading speed when they come to a word they don't know.

In order to make sure that students learn in the best possible way, I must remember that students differ in the way they learn, field dependent, field independent; right-brained, left-brained; visual, auditory, and kinesthetic; and they differ in their learning styles and intelligences as well. Therefore, to develop my students multiple intelligences and approaches to learning, I need to make sure I use a variety of teaching strategies (explanations, examples, and models of thinking). **As I begin to teach my lesson and, as I consider the effectiveness of my teaching during transition points in my lesson, I must check myself to make sure that I am teaching my students "how to think" as well as what to think.** If I can teach my students to think through situations, make adjustments in how they think about and solve problems, I can develop their ability and potential for learning.

**Assessing and Monitoring Student Progress (Principle 8)**

I need to know what and how my students are thinking, and whether they are learning what I am teaching throughout my lesson. So, the eighth teaching principle that I must learn and be able to use in my lessons is assessing and monitoring student progress. Assessing and monitoring students as I teach will ensure that all students are on the same page before continuing. I must monitor student progress closely and carefully early in the lesson so that I can find which students struggle with the material. I will assess my students at the start of the lesson, and while I am teaching, not just when I get finished teaching. Asking questions and making sure students understand, and providing ongoing assistance and monitoring all along the way, moves my teaching beyond the process of simply presenting or exposing students to material. I must also monitor my students while they are doing the written-work portion of the lesson so that I can provide feedback on what students have retained during the lesson. This way I will know whether all students understand the concepts. If I teach a lesson, do not assess and monitor my students along the way, and give them help at the point when they need it, I will end up either re-teaching them everything or allowing them to "fall through the cracks." **Assessing and monitoring my students at the start of the lesson, at transition points during the lesson, and at the end of the lesson will insure that students understand the material. I can then continue to develop their understanding as they progress through this lesson and beyond.**

**Providing Feedback and Reinforcement (Principle 9)**

Providing feedback and reinforcement to my students is also a critical part of effective teaching because it helps students improve their performance. Consequently, the ninth teaching principle that I will learn to use in my lessons is to provide feedback and reinforcement. Feedback is given to inform students about the accuracy and quality of their performance and to help students see areas where they need to improve whereas reinforcement is used to motivate students. Feedback is best used when it is given quickly, as soon as possible after assignments, and when it is specific. I must try my best to seek as many opportunities as possible to provide feedback, both to help my students, and to help myself because when I know where each student stands, I am in a better position to meet each student's learning needs.

Reinforcement is used to give praise or encouragement. Positive reinforcement is used to strengthen or promote a certain behavior by providing some type of reward and should encourage and motivate students. I will use positive reinforcement both to encourage learning and to encourage good behavior during the lesson. I will use feedback as much as possible and be very specific when using it and I will use reinforcement appropriately keeping in mind the age and maturity level of the student. In addition to ongoing feedback and reinforcement during my lesson, I will make a special effort to do so at transition points in my lesson. **Feedback and reinforcement when given consciously with a purpose and with consistency at transition points in my lesson will increase my students' knowledge of how well they are doing, and increase their motivation and potential for success in the next phase of the lesson.**

## Promoting Transfer of Learning (Principle 10)

The tenth teaching principle that I will learn to use in my lessons is promoting transfer. Since it is impossible and certainly not necessary to teach everything, promoting transfer of learning is very important. My students should be able to take their knowledge and skill from one situation and apply them in different situations. And, they should be able to see relationships and make connections between skills, concepts, and ideas. For example, when I teach students a skill such as how to locate words in a dictionary, they are learning how to learn, for the purpose of transferring this ability to their actual use of the dictionary as an essential learning tool. I must not assume that this transfer will occur automatically, however. Instead, I must help my students make the connection and apply this skill in their daily use of the dictionary.

As I teach I should remember that I always need to relate new material to the material I have already taught or material that the students already know and then extend their learning to new contexts. I must seek ways to relate material to the "real" world, to make students aware that what we study in our schools needs to be viewed within a cultural context, and to understand that there are multiple ways of knowing and different perspectives on the material we study. Since the curriculum that I will teach will center primarily on "mainstream" American culture, I can consciously build in transfer applications to other cultures. Spending more time learning a subject in depth will increase the chance that the students will learn it and that transfer to other contexts will be likely. **At transition points during the lesson, I will summarize and help students**

**make connections among points in learning. At the end of a lesson, I must provide closure and make sure students are able to state "what we learned and why it is important." Promoting transfer will occur primarily during the concluding phase of my lessons as we consider the relevance "Big Picture" and overall value and significance of each lesson.**

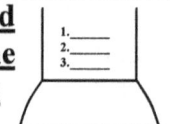

There are a variety of teaching methods that I can use to develop my lesson content. Some alternatives that I can choose from are direct instruction, cooperative learning, and inquiry learning, or simply direct and indirect teaching. My choice of method will made based on, "What is the most effective and efficient way to develop and deliver particular content, skills, and understandings to a particular group of students and insure that they learn?" These alternatives when combined with manipulative materials, meta-cognitive, and multi-sensory approaches can be effective and can promote even higher levels of learning.

Variety and appropriateness clearly pertain to the ten teaching principles. All ten of these teaching principles should be considered and incorporated appropriately into my lessons. Since teaching is decision making, however, it is unlikely that I will apply all dimensions of every principle in every lesson that I teach. Still, I should know the various dimensions of every principle, when and how to use them; and if I chose not to use certain performance indicators, I should know why. In all cases, I should not only be able to use the principle, but I should also be able to explain how and why I used specific dimensions of a principle in a particular lesson.

I know that including these ten teaching principles in every lesson will be difficult at first, but through conscious thorough learning of each principle combined with patient and careful practice, I will gain confidence. A major part of my teacher education at the university will include my ongoing reflections and the feedback and mentoring I receive from my supervisors. Therefore, as I proceed through the teacher preparation program, the quality of skillful precision teaching expected of all graduates will eventually become a natural part of my teaching style. I also know that continuing successful use of the principles and performance indicators of teaching effective culturally-transformative lessons will be a growth experience for me over a lifetime of teaching.

**The Organizing Framework and Lesson Agenda provide a coherent structure that makes it easy to incorporate the 10 teaching principles in my lessons so that they take on the form of a well-designed composition with introduction, development, and conclusion. For development, the Lesson Agenda provides an interactive sequence for me and my students to cling to during the lesson. These graphic organizers make it possible for me to create and deliver lessons with unity,**

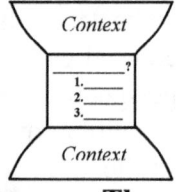

**continuity, and style—my style.** By establishing the lesson context, optimizing instructional time, using questions, providing clear instruction, assessing and monitoring student progress, providing feedback and reinforcement, creating a positive climate, maintaining positive behavior, promoting transfer of learning, and developing student thinking in my lessons, my students will learn more from my teaching. In addition, I will have a repertoire and the skill necessary to build a lifetime of masterful teaching.

This is teaching the **"THE CULTURALLY-TRANSFORMATIVE WAY"**

---

In the preceding description this beginning teacher illustrates the power and magnificence of culturally-transformative teaching. This teacher's plans for applying the teaching principles and organizers are exemplary. Surely this teacher has talent and potential, but already at the outset of her teaching career, she's becoming a star in learning what makes effective culturally-transformative lessons, and to use the teaching principles and performance indicators to think through her lessons. Descriptions from other teachers convey similar talent in their own unique teaching styles. The application of the scientific teaching principles in the multiple artistic and creative styles of so many classroom teachers that I have observed makes it clear that teaching is both a science and an art.

In the next section a set of procedures for managing lessons will take you from start to finish by giving you step-by-step directions to help you put it all together.

## Managing Culturally-Transformative Lessons: Designing, Planning, Implementing, and Reflecting on Lessons

Now that you know the basic components of culturally-transformative teaching and how you can integrate these components in culturally-transformative lessons, how do you plan for, implement, and reflect on lessons to enable this growing level of skill. Your successful use of the instructional management tools in this section will make each teaching opportunity a success and growth opportunity that enables you to know what to do and how to do it. In this section, the structure that is being provided is intended to give you a set lesson organizers for a lifetime of teaching. They will help you establish your approach to teaching, develop your own unique teaching style, and assure that your teaching meets the "best practice" standard.

Often teachers are attentive to the content they teach but they are less attentive to how they teach it to ensure that students learn it. Typically, only prospective or beginning teachers take the time out of necessity to thoroughly think through what they are going to do and these plans are inclined to be over-extensive. Others, who have been in a particular teaching situation for a while, are more inclined to teach whatever subject matter is outlined in the curriculum using the approach that seems sensible to them.

Culturally-transformative teaching calls for conscious thinking and it calls for brief but thoughtful planning on the part of both beginning and experienced teachers. It is purposeful well-reasoned teaching where few assumptions are made and little is left to chance. When you engage in this level of thoughtful planning and precise teaching, you are en route to becoming what Giroux refers to as a transforming intellectual.

The process for culturally-transformative teaching is simple and reasonable, and when learned and practiced consistently as you teach, it will eventually become second nature. This section gives you a template, a step-by-step process to help you prepare for culturally-transformative teaching so that your teaching is conscious, explainable, and effective. Not only will it work for you and your students, *you will know why and how it works and how to put it all together.* And your teaching will be predictable and replicable. You will be able to duplicate the performance in multiple contexts over the course of your teaching career. Isn't this what you want for the thousands of lessons that you will teach over a lifetime of teaching? I recommend that you follow the outlined steps in the five topics closely over the period that you are learning the process of culturally-transformative teaching. Then you can further refine and make this level of teaching your own as the steps of the process become integrated into your teaching style and repertoire.

The following directions will help you in carrying out five phases of teaching culturally-transformative lessons as follows: (1) Preparing/Designing the Lesson, (2) Developing the Lesson Plan, (3) Presenting the Lesson, (4) Implementing the Lesson, and (5) Reflecting on the Lesson.

## Preparing/Designing the Lesson

Begin the process of preparing for the lesson by thinking through what you want to teach, why you should teach it, and the most efficient and effective way to teach it. The following questions can help to guide your thinking:

- What is the relevance of the content to the lives of your students?
- Why should students learn it?
- How does the material relate to or not relate to the students' background knowledge and cultural experiences?
- What is the structure, the essence of subject matter knowledge (the big ideas) to be taught, and what are the critical attributes to be stressed in the lesson
- What is the transferability of skills, and concepts (The context; the bigger picture surrounding the content)?
- How can I represent the content from multiple cultural perspectives, ways of knowing?

- How can I target the content to develop student abilities, thinking, and application of knowledge, skills, and concepts?

It is at this phase in the process of thinking through your lesson that you are called upon to use your originality and creativity as you consider how you want to design and develop your lesson. The following steps in should help you through the process of designing the lesson:

**Step One.** Decide what you want students to know and be able to do at the end of your lesson. (Your Major Objective) Develop a lesson question to put your objective in the language of the students such as in the sample question: **What is symmetry?**

**Step Two.** Decide what is the best (most efficient and effective) way to be involved with students to assure that they learn and achieve the objective. Is it through direct instruction only or would you also use cooperative learning, or issue-oriented dialog?

**Step Three.** Consider the lesson arrangement and sequence of activities that you will provide—How students will get the necessary information (teacher input), how students will interact, receive assistance, and practice (interactive processing), and how students will show through (independent assessments) that they have learned, achieved the lesson objective and can answer the lesson question (accountability).

**Step Four.** Develop a skeleton outline/organizer/agenda for the sequence of activities in your lesson to engage students and anchor the lesson. Since the outline will be used with students, it should be stated in the language of the students with 3-4 key words to depict each event/phase of the lesson. See sample lesson outline below:

(Lesson Question) \_\_\_\_\_ _____ _____?
(Teacher Input)            1._____ \_\_\_\_\_ \_\_\_\_\_
(Interactive Processing)   2.\_\_ \_\_\_ \_\_\_\_ _____
(Independent Assessment)   3._____ \_\_\_\_\_ \_\_\_\_
Accountability

The lesson outline is useful in helping you design your lessons. You will find what is referred to here as the lesson ***outline/organizer/anchor/agenda*** serves as a useful tool in variety of teaching contexts; consequently, it is referred to here as a collective according to these four uses. In the planning stage, it is the Lesson Outline. In the teaching stage it is the Lesson Agenda used to introduce the lesson and it then serves as an anchor for the lesson while you teach. In all cases it is the organizer of your thinking, both as you plan and as you teach.

As the lesson planning outline, it helps you think with clarity about what you want to include in your lesson. For example, what is your main objective for the lesson? What is the main thing that you want students to learn? This objective is then turned into a question to structure your lesson phases, activities, or events. After you have decided on the lesson question, you can design the parts, ***events, activities, phases*** of the lesson to engage students in answering the lesson question. Sequence the lesson events, activities, or phases to enable you to develop students' thinking and learning as you teach and lead to them to fully answer the lesson question at the end of the lesson, ***lesson alignment***.

**Step Five.** Now that you have thought through and developed the outline for your lesson you can prepare a more detailed lesson plan to show how you will teach the lesson. The lesson outline is the skeleton for you to build on as you prepare your lesson plan. The lesson plan follows from the lesson question and the events, activities, or phases in the lesson. The lesson plan should contain sufficient detail for you to teach the lesson.

## Developing the Lesson Plan

Each institution, school district and school of education has its own lesson plan format and, of course, you obviously need to use the required format. However, you can adapt/adjust it to incorporate the following points in the format below so that the lesson conforms to the process in the Culturally Transformative Teaching Framework.

TITLE OF LESSON:
SUBJECT AREA:
GRADE LEVEL:
MATERIALS USED: Use visual, auditory, kinesthetic, and manipulative materials to address the learning and cultural styles of students.

DESCRIPTION: What is the context (Big Picture) for this lesson? Why should students learn it? What is the dominant/ non-dominant culture relationship? How will you extend students' learning? How will you prepare students to be successful?

OBJECTIVE: What is your lesson question? What specifically do you want students to learn?

PROCEDURES: How will you teach your lesson? Provide your sequence (step-by-step) to explain precisely what you will do. The series of events, activities, or phases of the lesson that you spelled out previously as part of your lesson design and agenda should be included here.

EVALUATION: What is your assessment of the lesson? Explain according to the Lesson Reflection guide which follows.

A word is in order here about lesson plans. I have stated previously that the planning process should be simple. Consequently, I would abbreviate the lesson plan. It is referenced here because prospective and beginning teachers believe that they need a detailed plan or script, something in their hands to refer to as they teach, and to prove to their supervisors that they are prepared to teach the lesson. These plans often lack constructive thought in terms of the essential big ideas that their students need to learn and they tend to be cumbersome and wordy—filled with educational jargon. The ability to engage in purposeful "on your feet" thinking is the quality that is most needed in teacher preparation programs. Teacher practitioners repeatedly acknowledge that over the long term, this type of long-form lesson plan is not sustainable.

Culturally-transformative teaching concentrates on teachers' *thought processes* prior to, during, and after teaching. Teachers may choose to write down whatever notes are sufficient and helpful to them at whatever stage they are in the process. Beginning teachers, or those beginning in the process, will obviously benefit from more detail.

The lesson outline/organizer/agenda is the tool for thinking through and conducting "on your feet" culturally-transformative teaching. When you get used to using it, your teaching will be manageable, easier, and more effective.

## Presenting the Lesson

As noted earlier, the lesson outline which you developed to plan the lesson now becomes the **_Lesson Agenda_**, the tool that you use to present and teach the lesson. *The lesson plan is for you; the lesson agenda is for the students.* When you introduce the lesson and present the lesson agenda to the students your make it their lesson as well, in the sense that students know what the lesson is about, how it will unfold, and what is expected of them. This simple organizer is the lesson in brief. It is episode three of the lesson framework and is so critical that its use in presenting the lesson is distinguished from its use in implementing the lesson. It is used at the beginning to introduce the lesson and its use continues throughout the lesson. The lesson agenda sets up and engages you and your students in the lesson.

The sample agenda for a third grade lesson which follows includes a lesson question and three events, activities, or phases. The number of events, activities, or phases will vary according to the lesson and your style of presentation, but all lessons should provide teacher input, interactive processing between you and the students, and student accountability, which in this case is the independent assessment.

(Lesson Question)  **What is Symmetry?**

(Teacher Input)  **(1) Think/learn with Ms./Mr._____**

(Interactive Processing)  **(2) Yes/No Activity**

(Independent Assessment)  **(3) Complete worksheet**
Accountability)

The agenda should receive a dramatic presentation and it should be used throughout the lesson to enable you and your students to keep pace with the lesson events and transition points between phases of the lesson.

## Implementing the Lesson

To expand on the lesson agenda, a full explanation of the lesson implementation process is detailed below. The implementation of your lesson involves using the Lesson Framework, the five teaching episodes were presented earlier under lesson components. Remember, the Lesson Agenda is to be written on the instructional board or chart as the visible outline/organizer/anchor/agenda to be presented at the beginning of the lesson and used throughout the lesson. All other teaching episodes of the framework are to serve as a guide for you. Referencing the Lesson Framework (depicted earlier under The Organizers of Culturally-Transformative Lessons). The five teaching episodes help you implement your lesson in the following ways:

**Introduce the lesson** by establishing set (the Context/Big Picture) for the lesson—questioning/explaining why should students learn this, what do they already know about it, how does it fit into the real world, other cultural orientations, etc. (Use novelty, flair, drama to capture students' interest and attention).

**To Begin:** Present the Lesson Agenda to students *orally and in writing*—Have it written on a chart or the board in advance, or as you gain more confidence and skill, you can write the agenda as you present it.

Give your expectations for student participation, behavior, and accountability—Use of materials, what you expect students to do during the lesson to demonstrate their thinking and learning, and to demonstrate what they have learned following the lesson.

**To Continue:** As you make a transition from one phase, activity, or event in the lesson to the next, pause at transition points. Refer students to the lesson agenda to focus on the lesson question and check student understanding. Ask, "How much of the lesson question can we answer so far?" Summarize and make connections among key points in learning comparing dominant and non-dominant culture references as appropriate.

*Transition points*, the interval between lesson events or phases should also be used to:

- Summarize and make connections among points in learning.
- Assess and monitor student understanding relative to background knowledge/cultural experiences
- Give feedback, praise, and encouragement to students.
- Structure changes in emphasis, topic, procedure, movement.
- Provide directions and set expectations for the next phase of the lesson.

- Consider your timing and effectiveness and change course if necessary.
- Stimulate attention and reinforce behavior and learning expectations.
- Assess student thinking and learning, and adjust teaching approach if necessary.
- Monitor the extent to which students can answer the lesson question.

Essentially, use transition points to take stock of the lesson and make adjustments as needed—re-teach if needed before moving on. Pause, make eye contact, and engage students. Build for smooth conceptual flow in points of learning.

**To End:** Summarize key concepts. Refer students to the Agenda and have students answer the lesson question. Debrief students on key points. Have students complete the written assessment.

**Conclude the lesson** by re-establishing the context (Big Picture)—How this lesson adds to students' store of knowledge. Review how the lesson relates to multiple cultures and multiple perspectives. How can the concepts and principles be applied in the real world to make a difference among the world's peoples? What more about the lesson content will students be learning in the future?

Each time you teach you are in a continuous state of reflection during the lesson about all aspects of the teaching. Are my students getting it? Did I set up the lesson fully or are students confused? Am I going too fast, too slow? What adjustments can I make now and what will I have to live with until the next lesson? Typically, there is no systematic way to pinpoint problems or successes. However with the lesson agenda, you have a built in opportunity to assess your performance at each phase of the lesson and you can usually make adjustments in-process when a redirection of the course you are on would matter most. Still, you should be attuned to needed changes from lesson to lesson as you teach. The tool for reflecting on the lesson serves as a guide to your thinking and planning.

## Reflecting on the Lesson

Lesson reflection makes teaching a growth-oriented process for each teacher. It takes conscientious, systematic, continuous day-to-day reflection to be and become a master teacher. Culturally-transformative teaching calls for ongoing reflection and change based upon your analysis and assessment. The culturally transformative lesson framework, teaching principles, and performance indicators provide the substance and process for you to become this master teacher, but your overall teaching effectiveness will depend upon your diligence in assessing your own progress and making incremental improvement with each lesson. A mentor or supervisor may be able to give you feedback, but you are the person who really makes the call and the appropriate change.

Effectiveness in teaching culturally-transformative lessons is dependent upon your engagement in reflection after each lesson. The following questions can be used:

What specific teaching principle(s) did you choose to focus on in this lesson?

How effective were you in using the lesson framework (agenda) and applying the teaching principles(s) in the lesson? Explain carefully.

- Based upon your lesson's design and implementation, how do you feel about your teaching effectiveness overall? Explain.

- Were you able to relate the material to other cultural orientations? Explain.

- Did your students effectively answer the lesson question?

- Did your students' accountability tasks show that students learned/met your expectations?

- What would you change?

Each of your lessons should show incremental growth in relationship to your ability to use the Lesson Framework and Agenda to apply the 10 teaching principles and 10 performance indicators in your lessons to develop your teaching skill.

This volume presents in a concise manner, a guide to teaching that you can use on your own or with assistance and coaching from a mentor. The process can be structured to develop your teaching skill over a series of lessons during a structured course as part of a teaching internship, or if you are already teaching, it can be used in a series of professional development sessions. Part Three explains how you can be supported and can grow in your ability to teach effective culturally-transformative lessons through mentoring and coaching in a growth-oriented supervision process.

**Positive Behavior**            **Positive Climate**

**Establishing Set**            **Optimizing Time**

_____?

**Clarity**

1. _____

     **Assessing/Monitoring Progress**

2. _____

**Using Questions**

3. _____

4. _____

     **Feedback/Reinforcement**

**Developing Thinking/Ability**            **Transfer**

# Part Three: Culturally-Transformative Teaching as a Professional Growth Activity

Part Three of this volume looks at the process of teaching culturally-transformative lessons as a growth-oriented undertaking in which teachers are concerned with getting better and better at what they do. Culturally-transformative teaching as a professional growth activity focuses on developing each teacher's skill in teaching effective culturally-transformative lessons through ongoing practice, coaching, and evaluation. This effort may seem daunting at first glance when looking at the competencies as they are explained in Part One, and the principles and performance indicators listed in Part Two, but the process overall is relatively simple. Teachers find the process to be logical and in conformity with their usual approach to teaching lessons. Even more, they find the results to be worthwhile in terms of their growing expertise in cultural and pedagogical knowledge and skill, and in terms of their growing ability to increase cross-cultural understanding and excellence in their students' learning.

## Basic Premises and Beliefs Which Guide the Process

The focus throughout this volume is on making it possible for teachers get better and better at what they do, always keeping the teaching of effective lessons at the center of what they do. The belief is that professional growth in teaching must be concerned with the dynamic process of "on-your-feet" teaching by letting teachers know what effective teaching looks like and helping them get better and better at it . Clearly though, supervision and evaluation are areas of teaching which can engender negative feelings among teachers as they think about their *bosses making judgments about them* rather than about their teaching of effective lessons. My conversations with teachers reveal that it's not so much that they fear supervision and evaluation. In fact, they welcome the support and confirmation of their teaching effectiveness. What they want is for the process to be substantive, to be based on their teaching, to be fair and equitable, and to be beneficial to them and their students.

The process that is outlined in this, Part Three of this volume, addresses these concerns. This volume considers the teaching of effective culturally-transformative lessons as an ongoing growth-oriented process. My interest in teaching culturally-transformative lessons stems from my belief that teaching is a process that teachers never fully master and that effective teaching is not a given that comes with certification. Knowing that as teachers we are all lifelong learners, my even stronger belief is that learning the principles of culturally-transformative teaching, the performance indicators, and their effective application in lessons is a goal worth continually striving for throughout our careers. Over time, competence with the methodology would be expected to reach a high threshold but, as students change, our ability to use the teaching principles and performance indicators to meet the diverse learning needs of our students will continue to be the "big challenge."

Flowing from this premise are other beliefs, which distinguish teaching for growth from teaching for evaluation, and which guide the process outlined in this volume of the professional development series. These beliefs are set forth below to serve as a guide for the process. Teaching effective culturally-transformative lessons for professional growth includes separating teaching for growth and teaching for evaluation, focusing on *teaching lessons* rather than broader more encompassing dimensions of classroom practice, using established agreed-upon criteria and procedures, giving teachers the opportunity to demonstrate their *best* teaching performance in a lesson for evaluation, and evaluating the *teaching* rather than evaluating the teacher.

- Teaching for growth is to be set apart from teaching for evaluation. Teachers, therefore, are supported and given the opportunity to work individually and together as colleagues and mentors to develop their skill in teaching and have their efforts and growth in teaching performance appraised by supervisory staff at the end of the process.

- The teaching of lessons (learning segments at the micro-level) is to be the focus of the growth process as opposed to using the teacher's ability to design instructional units as the source of instruction and evaluation, for example. The unit may be the source from which the lesson is derived and taught, but the interest in this growth process is on the teaching behavior used to teach the lesson.

- The process is to focus on *teaching as it occurs in the lesson* rather than with other dimensions of teaching (classroom practice) that comprise the teacher's overall performance in the school and classroom—promptness, cooperation, working well with parents, designing attractive bulletin boards, etc. While these areas are recognized as important, characterizations of these dimensions of teaching can be made through other formats.

- The criteria used to determine growth in teaching, and its supervision and evaluation, are to be based on theory, research, and evidence-based practice that is understood and supported by all parties, and conducted according to agreed-upon procedures by teachers and supervisors.

- Teachers are to know what is expected by supervisors and be given the opportunity to demonstrate *their best performance* when their teaching is being observed for evaluation.

- Supervisors who observe lessons are be to present for the full lesson. All phases of the lesson are important, particularly the introduction and conclusion.

- The interest in the professional growth process is to be in evaluating *teaching* rather than evaluating *the teacher*.

- Supervisors of teaching also need to be knowledgeable about the role and function of culturally-transformative teaching and committed to the beliefs and criteria that guide the growth process so that they can provide leadership and support to teachers throughout the process.

The process as it is outlined in this volume enables teachers to think through, establish goals and set up a teaching development plan that can help them address the learning needs and styles of a broad range of students. Successful student learning and the teachers' ability to teach powerful lessons with ease, as it will surely happen from day-to-day, will keep them striving to get better and better at teaching culturally-transformative lessons. When teachers operate from such a plan, the students will appreciate the attention they are receiving to help them grow in cross-cultural understanding and excellence in their learning.

## The Source and Rationale for Culturally-Transformative Teaching as a Growth Process

Culturally-transformative teaching as a professional development activity, as alluded to earlier, has quite a history and track record. The culturally-transformative lesson framework, teaching principles, and performance indicators have evolved over time. Teachers in numerous classrooms, both prospective and practicing K-12 teachers in both "mainstream" and culturally diverse classrooms at the university and elementary and secondary schools, have participated in the process. In each instance, the teachers found the process useful and easy to follow and their growth in teaching well worth the effort.

Some teachers, especially those with a special flair for creativity, found that the approach encouraged greater precision in their teaching. These creative teachers flourished with the process because it brought structure and predictability to their natural artistic flair in teaching. Similarly, teachers who were just beginning to learn how to teach and those who were struggling benefitted substantially from engaging in the process as well for they had a guide to refer to help them develop and improve their teaching methodology. Teachers who had been teaching for a while also took to the process. They described it as what effective teachers would seem to do naturally. Many teachers said that it's what all good teachers do but just haven't thought about or put a name to. One of these naturals even referred to the use of a three-step lesson agenda as the way she naturally organizes her lessons: In step one "I do," meaning I do the teaching—in step two, "We do," meaning, we both interact and practice together—In step three, "You do," that is, you show what you have learned through independent assessment and practice. The culturally-transformative dimension, however, was described as something new which few if any of the teachers had ever considered, but once they understood its rationale and application in lessons believed that the cultural component was very important.

## Looking Up Close at the Process

Teaching is a holistic complex dynamic interactive process so much so that teachers may wonder how it can be compartmentalized into discrete elements. Yet to make it possible for teachers to grow in the dynamic holistic process of teaching, it is necessary to isolate its attributes (the teaching principles and indicators of performance). Teachers can then focus on, analyze their behavior, and work to refine their performance. The model for teaching culturally-transformative lessons helps teachers think about and put a name to what they are doing while teaching so that it becomes conscious and replicable. They are therefore able to explain to others what they are doing, and why, and can repeat the behavior in the future. An important goal in isolating the attributes of teaching, is to develop a teaching mindset of metacognition, for teachers to consciously think about what they are doing in the act of teaching—the principles and behaviors that they are employing—and why, and to work continuously to refine their performance.

The Culturally-Transformative Teaching Model and accompanying instruments and guidelines are outlined in Part Two of this volume. Teachers will need to refer to Part Two throughout the professional growth process for it defines the process and contains the instructional elements and their uses in teaching. The teaching principles and performance indicators provide the substance and the instruments and guidelines help to facilitate the use of the principles and performance indicators in the lesson.

## The Professional Growth Sequence

The recommended professional growth process, when used for growth and evaluation with groups of teachers needs to be set up and carried out over a substantial expanse of time. During the dynamic process of teaching, teachers can focus on the teaching elements as outlined in the following stages:

1. Becoming proficient with the instruments, particularly the use of the teaching framework, lesson agenda, and the first four teaching principles: establishing set,

optimizing time, maintaining positive behavior, and maintaining a positive climate as the baseline for teaching. *These instruments and principles are basic and essential.*

2. After becoming skilled with the four base-line teaching principles it would be beneficial for teachers to obtain facility with employing the next four teaching principles: clarity, using questions, assessing and monitoring progress, and giving feedback and reinforcement in lessons.

3. Finally, it is useful for teachers to add the remaining two teaching principles: developing student thinking and transfer of learning, with the goal of finally putting it all together in an integrated performance. The Lesson Framework sequence is designed so that when teachers follow it closely as they teach, the teaching principles and performance indicators tend to flow into the lesson.

## Gaining Proficiency in the Process

Teachers are cautioned to be patient, however, for it will take concentrated practice to achieve facility in learning the process and in applying the principles. The model is simple, straightforward, efficient, and sure to be useful for teachers and their students, but it will take time for a level of comfort to set in with it. Teaching in any form is a complex series of behaviors, and focusing on individual principles and performance indicators will seem cumbersome at first because teachers are *giving conscious attention to the selected behavior(s)* while also employing other principles in their teaching. Those who have been teaching for a while will also find it challenging to change old habits. As with other forms of skill-based learning, to become proficient in culturally-transformative teaching, teachers need to practice long enough to integrate the framework and teaching principles into their teaching repertoire. As they practice, it is expected that they will experience varying degrees of comfort and discomfort as part of the growth process:

- The first few times of use and practice, they are likely to feel strange or awkward.
- After awkwardness passes, the next stage is one of feeling inauthentic or phony.
- In the next stage, they are likely feel more skilled but mechanical.
- Finally, as the skill becomes fully integrated into their teaching style, culturally transformative teaching starts to feel natural as they make it their own.

Diligence and commitment are necessary and ongoing feedback from others who also know the process, a colleague, mentor, supervisor, or consultant throughout the process is helpful. It is recommended that the following actions be taken:

- Engage in applying the teaching principle.
- Obtain feedback.

- Reflect on the feedback.
- Modify the performance and engage in the skill again and again until automaticity is achieved.

## The Professional Growth Process in Schools and Universities

Professional development and growth in culturally-transformative teaching as outlined in this volume is an important activity for *all* teachers, those who are just learning to teach and those who have been teaching for a while. Beginning teachers have the opportunity to learn effective teaching practice at the outset of their careers as part of their university's teacher preparation program and practicing teachers are able to reflect on the current status of their teaching and make refinements in their performance as part of the school's professional development program.

The professional growth activities to be shared in this part of Volume IV of the professional development series are designed to take place in two settings, at the university level and the school level.

- In each setting the activities are based on clearly defined criteria and a well-established sequence for implementation.

- Goal setting at the outset of the process and interim goal status and completion conferences occur in both settings at defined points in the process.

- Collegiality among peers and/or master teachers and cumulative documenting of teaching progress based on ongoing observations and feedback are the essence of the process in both settings.

- In both settings, the ongoing progression of working together as colleagues is geared toward each teacher's ultimate effectiveness in teaching culturally-transformative lessons as determined by his/her documentation in performance portfolios and demonstrations of teaching performance to supervisory staff at the end of the process.

Universities and schools are the institutions most concerned with developing quality teachers. The professional growth activities outlined in this section are designed to be implemented in ways that develop and enhance teaching effectiveness, specifically, teachers' cultural and pedagogical effectiveness in teaching culturally-transformative lessons. Universities through their teacher education programs, especially for those who are just beginning to enter the teaching profession, play the most essential role in assuring that teachers are prepared at the time of graduation to perform effectively for a lifetime of teaching in schools. The K-12 system of schools also have important roles to play in assuring that teachers retain their enthusiasm and continue to grow in their teaching skill and expertise.

Pre-service and in-service arrangements for schools and universities as they are described below are two examples of the ways in which the professional growth process has been workable in the unique circumstances these two settings. There are numerous equally valid ways in which the activities could be set up to conform to the needs of particular audiences and settings. In keeping with the belief of the series that there is no one best way to teach, there is no one best way to develop teachers who are effective in teaching culturally-transformative lessons. Adaptations to the process as outlined here are expected and welcomed.

Descriptions of the arrangements in these two settings also provide insight into the ways in which the teaching competencies and lesson design in Part One, and the teaching model in Part Two, came about. In the first instance at the school level, it reviews how the teachers learned the competencies and lesson design and how their work resulted in the teaching principles and performance indicators. In the second at the university level, it reviews how the teaching principles and performance indicators of the model were developed and can be implemented. The descriptions in both settings provide insights into the manner in which a collegial process of professional growth can occur in schools and universities under the guidance of a designated faculty member or a consultant who has worked through the process.

## Professional Growth in School Settings

Just imagine a school setting where there is overwhelming commitment and enthusiasm for educational excellence! My assignment, as educational consultant to the principal and teachers in this setting, was to open a new school and design an educational program with "state of the art" curriculum and instructional techniques. What an exciting "once in a lifetime" opportunity!

The school's world-class teachers began at the outset of working with me with eager interest in learning the qualities associated with cultural and pedagogical competence. The K-8 school served a predominantly Latin American population, and the teachers represented a variety of cultural backgrounds, a majority of whom were Latin Americans who wanted to foster both mainstream qualities, behaviors, and values and at the same time preserve the values and traditions of their culture of origin. They had the desire to be the "best" and carry out the school's mission as communicated by the agency's Board of Directors, the school's visionary executive director and its committed charismatic principal. We were recruited for just this purpose—to create a school of excellence and set the stage for the school to grow and flourish. I was asked to serve as educational consultant to design the educational program in all of its dimensions and help the teachers in their quest for excellence.

The school's teachers were dynamic and very creative throughout our work together over the course of five years. I learned as much from them as they did from me. I traveled to the school at intervals when it was convenient for the faculty to work with me. Visitations were more frequent and concentrated during the first year with one visitation extending as long as a month. In subsequent years, the visits tapered off to as few as three two-week visits. During these visitations at the beginning, middle, and end of the school year, the teachers were involved working with me in numerous workshop sessions learning the competencies that led to the Culturally-Transformative Teaching Model. This also included field testing the teaching principles, performance indicators, and lesson organizers. At this point culturally-transformative teaching was a concept yet to be refined to its present form. The Culturally-Transformative Teaching Model as it is presented in Part Two of this volume was an important outcome of the professional development efforts in this school.

The format for the work at this school included working with teachers as a group and as individuals in classrooms. The concepts and behaviors associated with teaching effective culturally-transformative lessons were developed in a large group session. Afterward, I had the opportunity to work individually with each teacher to observe lessons and give feedback on specific areas of performance, to demonstrate techniques, and just to enjoy being in the classrooms to acknowledge each teacher's success and growing ability in teaching culturally-transformative lessons. One of the teachers, for example, was unusually talented in his teaching, so much so, that I will always remember the quality of his work. It was impressive to see one lesson, in particular, where he gave a full and complete explanation and criteria for the task of writing poetry, then gave his students a time frame for working in four cooperative groups to create a poem, and finally, for each group to present its poem creatively and enthusiastically to the class—all within a 45 minute class period. What a talented teacher and what a talented class! Such performance is worth noting because even this gifted creative dynamic teacher appreciated the opportunity to learn and teach his lessons using the culturally-transformative method to give structure to his lessons and to substantiate and refine his considerable talent.

The school visitations outlined below describe the course of events for the first year of a five year commitment to develop, implement, and evaluate the four strands of the school's education program. In this volume the focus is primarily on the teaching strand. During this year, on-site visitations to the school took place in approximate three-month intervals. The principal was involved at the outset and in all aspects of designing and developing the program by providing the leadership and maintaining communication with me to discuss ongoing progress at the school throughout the year.

The sequence and process for working in the school with teachers to develop and implement the teaching process over the course of one year included the following events and activities:

**Orientation Prior to the Opening of School**

(First Consultant Visitation for One Month)

Orientation and training consisted of a one-month period of work with the faculty prior to the opening of school. During this time, the faculty received an overview of the areas and the ways that we would work together to accomplish the mission and goals of the school, the roles and responsibilities, and the process and time frame for our work. Even though effective classroom management was also a priority for us, during this orientation month, two weeks were spent learning about teaching and the direction it would take in the school. The results of these efforts are spelled out in Part One of this series, in the competencies and process for teaching effective culturally-transformative lessons.

Teachers were asked to set teaching goals for the year based on the competencies and outlined teaching process. They were also to include in their goals the ways in which they would work with other teachers over the course of the year to practice employing the competencies in their lessons and assist each other in achieving their goals. So, in addition to giving them the rationale for culturally-transformative teaching, providing basic information and demonstrating and modeling the competencies and teaching process, teachers had opportunities to practice and role play to display their growing understanding of culturally-transformative teaching. Their effective use of the lesson agenda was an important part of the process. I conducted every seminar session by modeling the culturally-transformative teaching process, always explaining what I was doing and why. Over the two-week period the teachers could readily see how they could apply the teaching competencies in their lessons.

**Follow-Up and Classroom Visitations**

(Second Consultant Visitation for Two Weeks)

During the two-month interval between visitations, I received reports from the principal about the work in progress and provided material to keep the teachers involved in the process. Fortunately during the first visitation the teachers and I achieved a high degree of trust and enthusiasm for working together; consequently, they looked forward to this second visitation.

I worked with the teachers as a group for one day to review the processes covered during orientation month and have them share their accomplishments. The remaining nine days were spent working in individual classrooms with each teacher to observe and coach each teacher in the dimensions of teaching, while at the same time, discussing the features of classroom practice in general. We wanted consistent classroom management procedures throughout the school so considerable time was spent coordinating and helping teachers make adjustments to the expected norm as needed. Over the two-week period, I had the opportunity to observe each teacher teaching one or more lessons and give them written feedback on the observation. We had worked extensively on using a lesson agenda during orientation month in our role playing and practice sessions, and many of the teachers had used the lesson agenda with their students consistently between my visitations and demonstrated that they could use it with relative ease. These teachers, of course, wanted more help with establishing the context and ways to make their lessons culturally-transformative. Their effective use of the agenda was an important first step for the teachers, a point of reference for extending our work to other competencies, and for conceptualizing the structure of culturally-transformative teaching.

**Follow-Up and Classroom Visitations Continued**

(Third Consultant Visitation for Two Weeks)

Now that most teachers had a working knowledge of the competencies and lesson agenda and sufficient time to practice lessons using the agenda as their lesson organizer, again, my role during this visitation was to have teachers share their accomplishments with me. In order to help them continue to progress in their skill development, I needed first to determine the extent to which they had followed through on recommendations from earlier visitations and had practiced employing the competencies in their lessons. My visitation, then, was centered on observing the lessons of teachers and giving them a written interim assessment of their performance indicating strengths and areas for development as preparation for the lesson demonstrations they were to give the principal and me during the final visitation for the year. Their portfolios—documenting their practice sessions, completion statements of their goals, and the artifacts to document their efforts—were also to be ready for review.

**Summary of Performance and Evaluations**

(Fourth Consultant Visitation for Three Weeks)

This final visitation for the year was our opportunity to review and celebrate our accomplishments in all areas of the education program and set a direction for the summer and coming year. The principal, who had been involved in all areas of constructing the school's education program, was heavily involved in this visitation. Together we reviewed all portfolios and observed the lessons of all teachers. Following the visitation we both wrote summaries from our perspectives of each teacher's performance in teaching based on the competencies and lesson design outlined in Part One of this volume. A report containing these summative evaluations was shared with the school's executive director and Board of Directors.

Because of the vast undertaking of the project in this new school with faculty who wanted assistance with the three classroom practice volumes in this professional development series: culturally-inclusive classroom management, a culturally-centered education program, and culturally-transformative teaching much more time and commitment on the part of the faculty were necessary than would typically be the case. In most instances, four visitations of one week each over the course of one year would be sufficient to help school faculties implement the Culturally-Transformative Teaching Model.

## Professional Growth in University Settings

At university settings professional growth activities related to actual teaching generally take place during the field experiences of the student intern's program of studies, where students practice teaching in the schools of the area. The goal is to assure that the interns learn how to teach. These experiences typically involve collaborative arrangements between the university and local schools for the period when the interns are placed in schools with mentor teachers to learn how teach in "real world" settings. The challenge in these placements is to make sure that there is agreement among all parties as to *what makes good teaching* and that the *substance and mechanics of the process* are spelled out in a manner that accomplishes both objectives. The professional development and growth process in this section is designed with both objectives in mind and to illustrate how other universities can use a similar approach.

The process began as a major initiative led the Department Chair of Curriculum and Instruction and the Dean and faculty of the College of Education who wanted to be sure that our students left the university as world-class teachers. This foresight and commitment from our department chair, in particular, to focus on teaching as its most important function led to the development of this model of culturally-transformative teaching. In fact, the Model for Teaching Culturally-Transformative Lessons included in Part Two of this volume, is a working example of the substance and mechanics for the student internship as they developed at this teacher preparation university.

Collaboration with university colleagues over an extended period led to the criteria and design of the Culturally-Transformative Teaching model. A very special university colleague helped to provide the leadership and coordination between the university and the five selected Teaching Center Schools who were the first to implement the model. We worked together enthusiastically and tirelessly with the students, teachers, and principals in the Teaching Center Schools over several semesters to set the standard for the process to be expanded to other schools in the community.

Deciding on the ten teaching principles and performance indicators of the teaching model was rather straight forward because we had the teaching theory and research and competencies to guide us and, as teaching practitioners ourselves, we were able to confirm that these were the key ingredients in teaching effective lessons, but then how to apply them in the lesson was a major hurdle to cross. With respect to designing the lesson, I had concluded after observing numerous lessons of both prospective and practicing teachers that most teachers were eager and wanted to do well, yet few teachers could conduct a task analysis to figure out what to teach, how to teach it most expediently and effectively within a given time frame, and be assured that students learn what they set out to teach. Oftentimes the activities in the lesson were unrelated to the lesson objectives and not in accord with the principles of learning. And even though many interns had rather elaborate lesson plans, and were enthusiastic, they seemed unable to connect with students and keep students working with them throughout the lesson. Many would just start teaching without setting the stage for what they were teaching or to check during the lesson to see if students were getting it. The goal very often was to get through the lesson activities rather than to have students learn something significant in the lesson. Considering these factors and others, it was clear in my mind that while having the teaching principles and performance indicators was a very important first step, we also needed to help our teachers design lessons and teach in ways that engage students in their lessons so they can be assured that students learn what is being taught.

The Culturally-Transformative Lesson Framework and Lesson Agenda became our most useful tools. My belief in using agendas as instructional tools stems from my own initial shortcomings in teaching. I found that after I faithfully put the series of subjects and lessons and what I wanted to accomplish for the day on the board and explained them, my students were eager to work with me. The stage was set for learning something significant each day! Volume Two, which focuses on classroom management, explains the use of the day's agenda.

Later as professor and supervisor of student interns, I noted one of my interns use a rudimentary version of the lesson agenda that is outlined in this series. After making this observation, I quickly recommended the approach to my other interns and then continued to expand and refine it to its present form. Now, both new and experienced teachers characterize the Lesson Agenda as their most useful teaching tool.

The contextual whole-part-whole nature of the Lesson Framework is derived from a variety of sources, most particularly from the educational literature on literacy. Its meaning and impact stems from the many lessons that I observed in which few if any teachers provided a background for their lessons and none mentioned the cultural viewpoint associated with the material even when the student audience was substantially different from the cultural viewpoint being conveyed. It was the lesson framework with its emphasis on contextual teaching that broadened my thinking and served as the catalyst for culturally-transformative teaching as outlined in this volume.

The instruments and guidelines, then, have quite a history. Essentially, they developed "in process" to facilitate applications of the teaching principles and performance indicators in the lesson. They serve as a guide to planning and teaching; they simplify and make lessons easier to teach; and they develop teachers' confidence in teaching to assure that students learn.

An explanation of competence in teaching culturally-transformative lessons is provided in Part One of this volume. The specific elements and mechanics of the model for conducting culturally-transformative lessons are set forth in Part Two. Samples of the forms and materials to help with the mechanics of culturally-transformative teaching are included in the Appendix at the end of this volume. These samples are designed to serve as a guide to help teachers, mentors, and supervisors implement the professional growth process in K-12 schools or university settings.

Professional growth, as considered in this part of the volume is accomplished at the university level in the following ways. Full semester class sessions and focused seminar sessions are arranged to enable interns to learn and practice employing the teaching principles and performance indicators in their lessons. The professional growth process begins as early as the junior year in the in the field experience sequence and is phased gradually into the internship where it becomes more comprehensive and highly focused. Interns are supported in learning how to teach culturally-transformative lessons by classroom professors, clinical professors who supervise students in their field placements, and lead teachers in the local schools of the area, who serve as mentors to the interns. In these arrangements interns learn the teaching principles and are able to put them into practice to help them get better and better at teaching. A sample proposed sequence for the Professional Growth Activities during the semester internship is as follows:

**Orientation Sessions for all Participants in the Process**

Orientation and training sessions conducted by university faculty for lead teachers in the schools are provided prior to the opening of school. All teachers who work with students during the internship are required to participate in these sessions during which they learn the ten teaching principles and performance indicators of culturally-transformative lessons from the vantage point of how they would demonstrate and give feedback to students on their performance.

Similar sessions are provided for interns. In these seminar sessions at the beginning of the semester interns learn about the substance and process of teaching effective culturally transformative lessons in a general way and expectations for performance during the semester are established. Sessions are also held to help interns learn how to videotape their lessons which are to be an essential artifact in the students' Document of Performance Portfolio.

After the orientation sessions clinical professors meet with interns and lead teachers in the schools to discuss the process in greater detail with more specifics. Forms and materials to help facilitate the semester-long process in the schools are distributed and explained. These materials give direction to the teachers and students as to how the activities are to take place in the schools.

**The Implementation Sequence in Teaching Center Schools**

The activities throughout the semester are both formative and summative and although some activities may be expanded to accommodate specific school situations, the sequence for all Teaching Center Schools includes these expectations.

At the beginning of the semester, interns establish goals and plans for applying the ten teaching principles and their performance indicators in their lessons over the course of the semester. They also make plans to videotape lessons to document their effectiveness in teaching culturally-transformative lessons. Interns teach seven lessons for observation and feedback by the lead teacher. They then have numerous opportunities to practice teaching for growth in the areas recommended by the lead teacher. At the middle of the semester interns teach a lesson to demonstrate their growth in teaching performance for evaluation by the clinical professor. At the end of the semester another demonstration of the interns' best performance is presented for evaluation by the clinical professor. At the same time, in a three-way conference with the lead teacher and clinical professor, interns submit and explain their Performance DVD and Document of Performance Portfolio to confirm their activities and accomplishments over the course of the semester.

Student interns are involved in the implementation sequence for one semester based on the university calendar and adjusted to the calendar of the participating schools as follows:

| | |
|---|---|
| Week 1 | Orientation Meetings. Interns develop Professional Growth Plans |
| Week 2 | Intern Placements in Schools; Interns Set up Document of Performance Portfolios—Their Goals and Plans for the Semester |
| Week 3 | Lesson Observation #1 |
| Week 4 | DVD Preparation and Portfolio Review |
| Week 5 | Lesson Observation #2 |
| Week 6 | |
| Week 7 | Lesson Observation #3 |
| Week 8 | Mid-Term Demonstrations of Performance and Evaluation Conferences |
| Week 9 | Lesson Observation #4 |
| Week 10 | DVD Preparation and Portfolio Review |
| Week 11 | Lesson Observation #5 |
| Week 12 | |
| Week 13 | Lesson Observation #6 |
| Week 14 | |
| Week 15 | Lesson Observation #7 |
| Week 16 | Final Demonstrations of Performance and Evaluation Conferences; DVD and Performance Portfolio Submitted |

The experiences in these two institutional settings influenced my thinking to the extent that many of the practices outlined in this four volume series evolved into and became what is now the Culturally-Transformative Teaching Model. This model came about as a result of my supervisory interactions with teachers in the act of teaching. The Culturally-Transformative Teaching Model, when placed in a growth-oriented professional development program, has tremendous potential for developing and improving teaching performance in both university and school settings.

# A Call to Action

My overwhelming passion for this volume of the series has to do with my assessment that teaching is the most important classroom function, yet the area most in need of improvement in our schools. This volume of the MASS Professional Development Series recognizes the necessity for teachers to teach full and complete lessons to assure that *all* students obtain the essential knowledge and the necessary skills for participating in the modern world, and for altering its course where necessary.

It is important as we come to the end of our work together in this volume to reflect on the meaning of this venture in teaching as a professional development activity. Of all the topics in this professional development series, teaching is the engine to make it all happen. Without effective teaching, the improvement of classroom practice in the other dimensions of this four-part Professional Development Series will continue to be elusive. From the competencies for teaching effective culturally-transformative lessons in Part One, to the Culturally-Transformative Teaching Model in Part Two, and the accompanying professional growth ventures as spelled out in this part of the volume, there is tremendous potential and opportunity for improving classroom practice through culturally-transformative teaching. Action is needed by its educational readers, its general readers, and its political leaders to act on the mission of making sure that effective teaching is provided to students of all cultural backgrounds as the highest priority for this nation. This volume makes the case for audiences, particularly universities and K-12 schools, to act on this priority. It emphasizes what is needed in terms of the necessary criteria, and it offers working models for putting the priority of teaching effective culturally-transformative lessons into action.

Clearly, though, teaching as discussed throughout this volume is but one strand of the improvement in classroom practice that is needed. The four volumes of the series connect the cultural context, culturally-inclusive classroom management, and a culturally-centered education program with culturally transformative teaching. They are all interconnected and all four volumes help its readers put it all together.

The diverse group of twelve classroom teachers, who we have followed through the series, was asked to address culturally transformative teaching, what it is, and how they can make their lessons more culturally- transformative. They responded accordingly:

## Classroom Teachers Talk It Over

"Culturally transformative teaching is taking dominant culture material and modifying it in the interest of truth and a broader world view. It seeks to help students find unity, logic, and broader meaning to what often comes to them as isolated bits of information, and to also consider the implications of what they are learning."

"Culturally transformative teaching is designed to make students think about other cultures in relationship to dominant culture material. This means that you connect what students of different cultures are learning with existing background information that is part of students' cultural experiences."

"Culturally transformative teaching occurs when we as teachers take what we are mandated to teach, change the ways in which we present information in efforts to help students take what they learn in the classroom and apply it to the outside world. It begins with setting up the lesson by embedding it in a real-world context, teaching the lesson thoroughly by integrating new learning with context, and concluding the lesson by transferring what was learned to the real-world context."

"Making lessons culturally transformative is all about making connections. If we can help students make connections and find their own unique meaning in the lesson, we are on the road to becoming successful."

"The idea of macro and micro objectives caught my attention in relationship to transformative teaching. I think of macro objectives as outside of school and micro as in school (more like field independent, detail driven)."

"If we can make the right connection between what students learn in school to relevant societal issues, we can enlighten students philosophically (taking into account the critical pedagogy cycle of learning-relearning-unlearning), to broaden, and transform the horizons of our students."

"Culturally transformative teaching is an opportunity for teachers to convey cultural awareness, knowledge, and even acceptance of others to students. The teacher as leader is in a unique position to impart these attributes to others. The teacher must first consider herself as "part" of our global culture and also desire to be a life-long learner in order to pass along cultural information to others. As for lessons being culturally transformative we have spoken of many ways to take the mapped-out curriculum and find ways to interpret and incorporate other cultures' material into the learning expectations. Sometimes ignorance is what keeps us from teaching in culturally transformative ways."

"Culturally transformative teaching is about making connections from what students already know to what they are learning beyond the dominant culture. I liked the framework which called for whole-part-whole contextual teaching—providing the cultural context for the material to be learned, using an agenda to teach the lesson, and helping students connect and transfer their learning to a broader real-world context. The use of the lesson agenda encourages thorough and precise teaching by promoting student engagement, maximizing instructional time and providing feedback to students about their learning."

"The professional growth process would have been so helpful to me when I did my student teaching. I don't think that I had enough guidance. The teaching principles would let me know what makes good teaching. It would also be nice if I had more help working with teachers at my school on teaching strategies. I really like this model."

---

As you conclude this volume, think about the characteristics of teaching culturally-transformative lessons as described by these classroom teachers. Be ready to provide your version and to demonstrate how you will teach in culturally transformative ways.

## A Summary of Learning in Volume IV

The volume was designed to help you implement the Culturally-Centered Curriculum from the preceding volume in a manner that builds cross-cultural understanding. It makes the point that it is the quality of teaching that makes the difference especially when faced with the omnipotent dominant culture—the "culture of power."

This volume of the series focused on the complex process of teaching a lesson in a manner that transforms learning from the dominant culture perspective toward embracing and taking on the perspectives of multiple cultures with the goal of building cross-cultural understanding. It concentrated on summarizing and explaining the theory and research associated with the competences, teaching principles and performance indicators and explained how they can be used in teaching a culturally transformative lesson. The volume also described useful tools for developing culturally- transformative lessons through step-by-step procedures for designing, planning, implementing and reflecting on lessons. To help teachers grow in the process of culturally-transformative teaching a growth-oriented process of formative and summative evaluation is outlined to conclude the volume. In review, some specific points are:

- The volume explained what culturally-transformative teaching is, and how it influences curriculum implementation, cross-cultural understanding, and classroom practice. Culturally-transformative teaching as a comprehensive approach is directed toward accomplishing the goal of developing cultural-competence in understanding, planning, and delivering dominant-culture curriculum. The process outlines twelve teaching competencies and shows how they interact in a lesson. The teaching model puts the process into a lesson framework, research-based set of teaching principles, and performance indicators which combine in lessons to promote student learning. Culturally transformative teaching is essential to accomplishing the series' intent of providing purposeful and explicit teaching to achieve optimum academic and affective student learning.

- The volume discussed the teacher effectiveness, cognitive theory, and critical pedagogy theory, and the way in which this literature serves as the background for culturally-transformative teaching. Teaching for understanding and application as emphasized in these theories is critical to culturally-transformative teaching.

- The volume focused on culturally-transformative teaching, as a comprehensive approach, centered on direct/explicit teaching while also incorporating other interactive approaches including cooperative learning and issue-oriented dialog. These approaches help achieve classroom practice goals, promote excellence in student learning, and build cross-cultural understanding.

- This volume introduced the components of the culturally-transformative teaching model, including the lesson framework and agenda, the ten teaching principles, and performance indicators. These principles and indicators relate to the identified theory, research and "best practice" in teaching, and when integrated into the Lesson Framework for Transformative Teaching offer a pedagogically sound approach to teaching a lesson that is both practical and effective.

- The volume presented the tools for effective culturally-transformative teaching—how to design, plan, implement, and reflect on your lessons. A detailed step-by-step approach has been offered to help put effective lessons together from start to finish.

- Culturally-transformative teaching was explained briefly in Part Three as a professional development activity that can be used effectively in as a complete pre-service or in-service program to help teachers grow in their ability to teach culturally-transformative lessons. It is "teacher friendly" and has been has been used successfully with both prospective and practicing teachers. Both teachers and principals benefit from using the process as part of the supervision process.

The structure of carefully crafted lessons is obviously an inherent component of effective classroom practice. Teaching for understanding and application through culturally-transformative teaching is emphasized because of its comprehensiveness in systematically teaching teachers how to teach in culturally competent transformative ways. The recommended principles and approaches are important because teaching to build cross-cultural understanding is too important to be left to chance as could be the case with indirect approaches. Now that we have looked closely at the ideas presented, teachers should be able to apply the culturally-transformative teaching process to develop their own teaching style, recognizing that it will take time, practice, and support to become proficient in its use.

## Opening Scenario (Afterthoughts)

What is your assessment of the teacher's teaching style based on your study of this volume? Please give examples to explain some specific insights that you gained from your study that you would recommend to this teacher.

## Questions/Activities

1. In what ways are the teaching strategies in this volume a support to classroom practice? What implications does this have for the way that you plan to conduct your classroom?

2. Explain how the teaching competencies in Part One contribute to effective culturally-transformative teaching. Compare your teaching with these competencies. Would you include other competencies? Please share your thoughts.

3. Explain the Culturally-Transformative Lesson Framework, how it follows a whole-part-whole sequence by beginning with the "big picture," then to the lesson segment, then returns to the "big picture," and the ways in which this approach promotes meaningful and applicable learning.

4. Explain the following concepts in relationship to the dominant mainstream culture and other cultures:

    Direct/indirect teaching    culturally-transformative teaching
    teaching principles         performance indicators

5. Describe the five episodes of the Lesson Framework for Culturally Transformative Teaching. How can your use of this framework serve as the tool for transforming knowledge beyond the dominant mainstream culture.

6. In what ways can the lesson framework, ten teaching principles, and performance indicators contribute to your success as a culturally-competent classroom teacher?

7. Explain in detail how the professional growth activities in Part Three can be implemented at your university or school.

8. Summarize the new ideas, principles, and concepts that you learned in this volume. Explain how you will implement them in your classroom.

Cooperative Group Activity:

Learn the process of culturally transformative teaching in the following manner:

- Become familiar with the 10 principles of teaching and performance indicators,
- Explain their application in teaching a lesson according to the Lesson Framework for Culturally Transformative Teaching and the Lesson Agenda
- Work in teams of two to design and plan to teach a simple lesson designed to promote cross-cultural understanding.
- Present the lesson in a group session with the group members as audience.
- Provide your reflection on the lesson with additional feedback from your group members.
- Teach the lesson to a group of "real" students in a K-12 classroom.

## Looking in Classrooms

Visit a school in your area for the purpose of finding out how the teachers teach in relationship to what you have learned in this volume. Observe and note the following.

(Ask questions of the teachers in areas where you need clarification):

1. What teaching strategies do the teachers employ and are all cultures embraced through the techniques employed?

2. How successful are students in learning the objectives of the teachers' lessons? How do you know?

3. How will you teach differently using the teaching framework (agenda), teaching principles, and performance indicators?

Following your visitation, write a brief Descriptive Summary Statement to explain what you observed about teaching in this setting. How does it relate to what you learned in this volume?

# Recommendations for Further Reading

Brophy, "Successful Teaching Strategies for the Inner City Child." *Phi Delta Kappa*, 1982, 63, 527-530.

> Brophy, a pioneer in teaching effectiveness, points to a number of instructional strategies which are also set forth in the culturally transformative teaching as being appropriate for the inner city child.

Cruickshank, D., D. Jenkins, and K. Metcalf. *The Act of Teaching,* 4th ed. Boston: McGraw-Hill, 2007.

> Cruickshank, Jenkins, and Metcalf summarize the research on K-12 teaching generally. Chapter eleven focuses narrowly on teaching, and provides background for the skills associated with culturally-transformative teaching.

Good, T. and J Brophy. *Looking in Classrooms*, 8th ed. New York: Addison Wesley Longman, Inc., 2000.

> Good and Brophy provide a thorough presentation and analysis of what goes on in classrooms. Much of their research and recommendations on teaching explain in detail some of the principles incorporated in culturally transformative teaching.

Perkins, D. and T. Blythe. "Putting Understanding Up Front." *Educational Leadership* (1994), 51 (4), 4-7.

> Perkins and Blythe emphasize that understanding is the goal of teaching effectiveness. This emphasis was an important step in developing the culturally transformative teaching model.

Rosenshine, B. "Teaching Functions in Instructional Programs." *The Elementary School Journal* (1983), 83, 335-351.

> Rosenshine's teaching functions are historic in setting the stage for systematic teaching. This article helps to explain the relationship between the teaching functions and culturally-transformative teaching.

# APPENDIX

*Rubric for Effective Culturally-Transformative Lessons*...94

*Document of Performance Portfolio*...95

*Lesson Observation Checklist*...96

*Teaching Performance Observation Report*...97

*Designing the Lesson*...98

*The Lesson Agenda*...99

*Teaching the Lesson*...100

*The Lesson Plan*...101

*Reflecting on the Lesson*...102

# Rubric for Effective Culturally-Transformative Lessons

The lesson is relevant and meaningful and age-appropriate with the students' background knowledge, diverse cultural perspectives, and interests in mind.

       Below Standard---------Developing Standard---------Meets Standard---------Exceeds Standard

Content knowledge is evident in a thoughtfully designed lesson plan. Procedures and materials are appropriate for achieving the lesson objective(s).

       Below Standard---------Developing Standard---------Meets Standard---------Exceeds Standard

The context for the lesson is established so that students understand the Big Picture, why the lesson is important, how it relates to the real world, how it addresses students' diverse cultural perspectives, how it builds on what students have learned previously, and how it will add to their future learning.

       Below Standard---------Developing Standard---------Meets Standard---------Exceeds Standard

An agenda (overview) of the lesson is used to introduce the lesson orally and in writing. The agenda includes the lesson question (main objective) and the parts of the lesson. The introductory comments give expectations and accountability for student participation and learning.

       Below Standard---------Developing Standard---------Meets Standard---------Exceeds Standard

The lesson is well managed with attention given to clear vision and control of the instructional setting, student seating, transitions and movement, student focus and attention, accessible teacher and student materials.

       Below Standard---------Developing Standard---------Meets Standard---------Exceeds Standard

The lesson is implemented effectively in sequence with appropriate timing and momentum, smooth transitions between parts of the lesson. Debriefing and summaries are used to assess the level of understanding and to highlight, reinforce, and integrate the key learning concepts.

       Below Standard---------Developing Standard---------Meets Standard---------Exceeds Standard

The content is fully taught giving attention to multiple cultural perspectives, critical attributes of the content, and the processes for learning the content (thinking skills, problem solving, use of visuals, technology…)

       Below Standard---------Developing Standard---------Meets Standard---------Exceeds Standard

Student success and accountability for learning is orchestrated during and at the end of the lesson by seeking the full involvement of all students through discussion, questioning and responding, cooperative groups, warmth, positive reinforcement; providing ongoing assessment through student demonstrations, correctives, work samples…..

       Below Standard---------Developing Standard---------Meets Standard---------Exceeds Standard

The lesson objective is achieved. Students can answer the lesson question by summarizing and explaining what they learned and its significance.

       Below Standard---------Developing Standard---------Meets Standard---------Exceeds Standard

The lesson is concluded by reestablishing the context, having students state what they learned and its relationship to the Big Picture, how it relates to other cultural contexts, added to their previous learning and will contribute to future learning.

       Below Standard---------Developing Standard---------Meets Standard---------Exceeds Standard

# Document of Performance Portfolio
# Contents for Parts I-II of the Performance Portfolio

**Part I**

Your lessons to include the following four items sequenced by the dates taught:

- The Lesson Plan and Agenda

- The Lesson Reflection

- Observation Checklist

- Observation Report

**Part II**

Your report of growth in using the lesson framework to apply the ten (10) teaching principles in lessons…

Summary of how you studied, practiced, taught, and reflected on your performance throughout the semester/year…

---

Have the portfolio ready for periodic review and to hand in at the end of the semester/year.

Please Note:
The presentation DVD is to be submitted at the end of the semester.

# Lesson Observation Checklist

**Suggested Rating:**   (3) strongly evident   (2) somewhat evident   (1) not evident

**Make notes on form of specific points for feedback.**

**Episode One.** Provide a context (introduction) for the lesson:

___Gained attention through novelty; material broader in scope than the lesson
___Activated/Developed student background knowledge.
___Gave the rationale and purpose for the lesson.
___Provided a cultural orientation for the lesson.
___Connected the lesson to common "real world" experiences; other cultural orientations
___Showed how the lesson content relates to the broader curriculum, previous learning, and will add to future learning.

**Episode Two.** Begin the lesson:

___Set expectations for using materials, participating, behaving, and overall accountability.
___Presented the lesson agenda (orally and in writing): The lesson question/objective and the sequence of lesson activities.

**Episode Three.** Teach according to the lesson agenda:

Built toward answering the lesson question assuring to include:
(1) teacher input,
(2) interactive processing and scaffolding, and
(3) independent assessment for student accountability.

**Episode Four.** Manage the Lesson by using transition points between lesson activities to:
-Summarized and made connections among points in learning.
-Assessed and monitored student understanding relative to
 background knowledge/cultural experiences.
-Gave feedback, praise and encouragement to students.
-Structured changes in emphasis, topic, procedure, movement.
-Provided directions for the next activity.
-Considered lesson timing and effectiveness and changed course when necessary.
-Stimulated attention and reinforced behavior and learning expectations.
-Assessed student thinking and learning, and adjusted
 teaching approach where necessary.
-Monitored the extent to which students could answer the lesson question.

**Episode Five.** Reestablish the context (conclusion) for the lesson:

___Had students share what they learned, why it is important, and how it relates to them and can be applied in other cultural contexts and situations.
___Showed how the new learning adds to what students already knew and will add to future learning.

# Teaching Performance Observation Report

**Teacher**_____  **Subject**_____
**Observation#**_____  **Grade**_____
**Level**_____
**Date/Time**_____  **Lesson**_____
**Focus**_____

**Strengths of the Lesson:**

**Areas of Growth (Since Previous Report):**

**Areas for Development**

# Designing the Lesson

**1.** Decide what you want students to know and be able to do at the end of your lesson. (Major Objective)

Develop a lesson question to put your objective in the language of the students. See Sample Question: **What is symmetry?**

**2.** Decide what is the best (most efficient and effective) way to be involved with students to assure that they learn and achieve the objective—the teaching model you will use—direct or facilitative teaching.

**3.** Consider the lesson arrangement and sequence of activities that you will provide—How students will get the necessary information (teacher input), how students will interact, receive assistance, and practice (interactive processing), how students will practice on their own (independent practice)—and how students will show that they have learned, achieved the objective and can answer the lesson question (accountability).

Consider relevance and appropriateness, and your level of knowledge and accuracy in preparing what to teach and how to teach it (pedagogical content knowledge).

Design each activity to align with and engage students in answering the lesson question and sequence activities to assure that students will be able to answer the lesson question at the end of the lesson. (Lesson alignment)

**4.** Develop a skeleton outline for the sequence of activities in your lesson. (See Sample Outline/ Lesson Agenda) Choose either the direct or facilitative teaching model to appropriately address your lesson question.

**5.** Now that you have developed the skeleton for your lesson you can prepare a more detailed lesson plan to show how you will teach the lesson using the recommended University format.

*Note: The lesson skeleton outline becomes the lesson agenda when you implement your lesson.*

# The Lesson Agenda

(Objective Question)           **What is Symmetry?**

(Teacher Input)                **(1) Think/learn with Ms./Mr._____**

(Interactive Processing)       **(2) Yes/No Activity**

(Independent Practice)         **(3) Practice with worksheet**

(Student Accountability)       **(4) Debriefing**

# Teaching the Lesson

**Introduce the lesson** by establishing set (the Context/Big Picture) for the lesson—why should students learn this, what do they already know about it, how does it fit into the real world, other cultures, etc. (Use novelty, flair, drama to capture students' interest and attention).

---

**To Begin:** Present the lesson outline (Agenda) to students **orally and in writing**—Have it written on the board in advance, or as you gain more confidence and skill, you can write the agenda as you present it.

Give your expectations for student participation, behavior, and accountability—Use of materials, what you expect students to do during the lesson to demonstrate their thinking and learning, and to show you that they have learned following the lesson.

**To Continue:** As you go through from one activity to the next in the lesson, pause and refer students to the lesson agenda to focus on the lesson question (How much of the question can we answer so far), to summarize and make connections among key points in learning and check student understanding.

Transition points between lesson activities may also be used to alert, give directions, and set expectations for the next activity in the lesson, to give feedback, praise and encourage students, consider your timing and effectiveness.

Essentially, use transition points to take stock of the lesson and make adjustments as needed—re-teach before moving on if needed. Pause, make eye contact, and promote student engagement. Build for smooth conceptual flow in points of learning.

**To End:** Summarize key concepts. Refer students to the Agenda and have students answer the lesson question. Debrief students on key points.

**Conclude the lesson** by re-establishing the context (Big Picture)—How this lesson adds to students' store of knowledge. What more about it they will be learning in the future, and how the concepts and principles can be applied and transferred to other situations, etc.

# The Lesson Plan

TITLE OF LESSON:
SUBJECT AREA:
GRADE LEVEL:

MATERIALS USED: Use visual, auditory, kinesthetic, and manipulative materials to address the learning and cultural styles of students.

DESCRIPTION: What is the context (Big Picture) for this lesson? Why should students learn it? What is the dominant/ non-dominant culture relationship? How will you extend students' learning? How will you prepare students to be successful?

OBJECTIVE: What is your lesson question? What specifically do you want students to learn?

PROCEDURES: How will you teach your lesson? Provide your sequence (step-by-step) to explain precisely what you will do. The series of events, activities, or phases of the lesson that you spelled out previously as part of your lesson design and agenda should be included here.

EVALUATION: What is your assessment of the lesson? Explain according to the Lesson Reflection guide which follows.

# Reflecting on the Lesson

### (To Be Completed After You Have Taught Your Lesson)

What did you think about <u>as</u> you were teaching?

Based upon your lesson's design and implementation, how do feel about your effectiveness overall. Explain.

Did your students effectively answer the lesson question?
Did your students' accountability tasks show that students learned/met your expectations?

What would you change?

For your next lesson, review the <u>Designing Your Lesson</u> and <u>Preparing to Teach Your Lesson</u> materials, keeping in mind your reflections on this lesson in relationship to the 10 Teaching Skills and the 10 Performance Indicators for each lesson, and aim of incremental growth and progress with each lesson.

# The MASS Professional Development Series in Review

Throughout the four-volume series the concern has been to set forth principles, strategies, explanations, and examples to improve classroom practice in ways that promote excellence in student learning. Educational excellence, as emphasized in each volume of the series, is dependent upon having a broader view of schooling than the traditional western-oriented view. Consequently, the twin goals of building cross-cultural understanding and promoting excellence in student learning are closely linked in this professional development series.

In the desire to improve the quality of education by pushing harder and mandating tests to assure dominant-culture learning, school officials have overlooked what is so obvious to those who are on the outside of this culture looking in. Clearly, the authorities have been going about it in the wrong way, with the wrong paradigm. The dominant mainstream American culture, upon which American classrooms operates, excludes other cultures and ways of viewing the world to the extent that many students see themselves as outside of the system. The series explains why many of these students are reluctant to fully embrace what goes on in American classrooms.

The limitations that have been placed on classroom practice in American schools have been revised and extended in the classroom practice sequence of this four-volume series which outlines culturally-compatible practices in classroom management, the education program and the teaching process. Each of these volumes discusses in detail with easy to understand step-by-step procedures, clear strategies and models to present in the simplest manner possible, ways to apply the principles and concepts in classrooms. Each is to serve as a distinct entity in terms of its focus and coverage of a strand of classroom practice, so that readers can select one or more volumes on their topics of interest. However, to obtain a complete picture of the strategies and methods associated with culturally-compatible classroom practices, readers should consider all volumes in the series.

This volume, the fourth and final in the series, made it clear that truth and accuracy in classroom practice are a must if there is to be credibility in schooling and excellence in learning. As a result it concentrated on transforming "what is" toward truth and accuracy in a broader world-wide context. It presented a comprehensive explanation and model for teaching in culturally-transformative ways to build cross-cultural understanding and assure excellence in student learning. It built on many of the points made in the culturally-centered education program outlined in Volume III by describing the competencies, procedures, and thought processes involved in the act of culturally-transformative teaching. The lesson Framework and the teaching principles combined with the professional growth process, that are laid out in this volume gave beginning teachers and teachers who are continuing in the field a growth-oriented systematic approach and model of teaching to use to elevate their thinking and broaden dominant culture material over a lifetime of teaching.

Even though the cultural phenomenon has been highlighted in these four volumes, it surely becomes clear to readers over the course of the series, that culturally-compatible classroom practice is simply effective classroom practice. It benefits students from non-dominant cultures but it benefits mainstream American students even more. Moreover, application of the recommended classroom practices does not require radical change in what is already established as fundamentally sound classroom practice. The necessary change stressed in each volume of the series, is to have teachers become "transforming intellectuals" who think about and analyze what they do, and then act in accordance with truth, accuracy, and openness in the interest of all students.

The MASS (Model Alternative School Services) *Professional Development Series for Excellence in Teaching and Learning* sets forth a coordinated approach for examining and improving classroom practice. MASS, through its publications and assistance is thorough and comprehensive in providing materials and services based in the needs of individual clients and schools.

This professional development series offers principles and strategies to help teachers learn conceptually how to build cross-cultural understanding and encourage excellence in student learning. Whether it is classroom management, the education program, the teaching, or all three of these classroom practice strands, MASS consultants are prepared to help teachers put the conceptual learning derived from the series into action in their daily classroom practice.

Contact us at www.schoolin.org

# References, Vol. 1-4

Adler, Mortimer J. *The Paideia Proposal, An Educational Manifesto.* New York: Macmillan, 1982.

Anderson, James D. *The Education of Blacks in the South, 1860-1935.* Chapel Hill: University of North Carolina Press, 1988.

Anderson, L. M.., N. L Brubaker, J, Allerman-Brooks, and G. Duffy. "A Qualitative Study of Seatwork in First-Grade Classrooms." *Elementary School Journal* (1985) 86, 123-140.

Anderson, Richard C., Elfrieda H. Hiebert, Judith A. Scott, and Ian A. G. Wilkinson. *Becoming A Nation of Readers: The Report of the Commission on Reading.* Washington D.C., 1985.

Apple, M. *Official Language: Democratic Education in a Conservative Age.* New York: Routledge, 1993.

Baloche, Lynda. *The Cooperative Classroom: Empowering Learning.* Upper Saddle River, New Jersey: Prentice Hall, 1998.

Bandura, Albert. *Self Efficacy: The Exercise of Control.* New York: Freeman, 1997.

Bandura, Albert. *Social Foundations of Thought and Action: A Social Cognitive Theory.* Upper Saddle River, New Jersey: Prentice Hall, 1986.

Bandura, Albert. *Social Learning Theory.* Upper Saddle River, N.J.: Prentice Hall, 1977.

Banks, James. *An Introduction to Multicultural Education.* Boston: Allyn and Bacon, 2002.

Banks, James. "Multicultural Literacy and Curriculum Reform," *Educational Horizons,* 69 (3), 135-140.

Banks, James, McGee, and C. Banks, eds. *Multicultural Education: Issues and Perspectives*, Hoboken, NJ: Wiley, 2004.

Bennett, Christine I. *Comprehensive Multicultural Education, 6th ed.* Boston: Pearson Education, 2007.

Berger, Eugenia H. *Parents as Partners in Education: Families and Schools Working Together.* Upper Saddle River, Inc.: Pearson, Merrill, Prentice Hall, 2004.

Bergstrom, A., L. M. Cleary, and Peacock. *Seventh Generation: Native Students Speak About Finding the Good Path.* Charleston, WV: ERIC Clearinghouse on Rural Education and Small Schools, 2003.

Berlin, Ira. *Many Thousands Gone: The First Two Centuries of Slavery in North America.* Cambridge MA: Harvard University Press, 1998.

Bloom, Benjamin S. *Human Characteristics and School Learning.* New York: McGraw-Hill, 1976.

Bloom, Benjamin, ed. *Developing Talent in Young People.* New York: Ballantine Books, 1985.

Brophy, Jere. "Successful Teaching Strategies for the Inner City Child." *Phi Delta Kappa* (1982) 63, 527-530.

Brophy, Jere. "Synthesis of Research on Strategies for Motivating Students to Learn." *Educational Leadership* (1987) 45, 2, 40-48.

Brophy, Jere. and M. McCoslin. "Teachers' Reports of How They Perceive and Cope with Problem Students." *Elementary School Journal* 93, 1 (1992): 3-68.

Brown, Dee. *Bury My Heart at Wounded Knee: An Indian History of the American West.* New York: Holt, 1970.

Bruer, John. *Schools for Thought.* Cambridge, MA: MIT Press, 1993.

Bruner, Jerome S. *The Culture of Education.* Cambridge: Harvard University Press, 1996.

Bruner, Jerome S. *The Process of Education.* Cambridge Mass.: Harvard University Press, 1963.

Charles, C. M. *Building Classroom Discipline.* Boston: Allyn and Bacon, 2002.

Charles, C. M. *Essential Elements of Effective Discipline.* Boston: Allyn and Bacon, 2002.

Chester, M. D. and B. J. Beaudin. "Efficacy Beliefs of Newly Hired Teachers in Urban Schools." *American Research Journal* 33, 1 (1996): 233-257.

Clayton, J. B. *One Classroom, Many Worlds: Teaching and Learning in the Cross-Cultural Classroom.* Portsmouth, NH: Heinemann, 2003.

Coleman, Daniel. *Emotional Intelligence.* New York: Bantam Books, 1995.

Coleman, Michael C. *Presbyterian Missionary Attitudes toward American Indians, 1837-1893.* Jackson: University of Mississippi, 1985

Coloroso, Barbara. *Kids are Worth It.* New York: Harper Collins. 2002.

Cremin, Lawrence. *American Educator: The Colonial Experience 1607-1783.* New York: Harper and Row, 1970.

Cremin, Lawrence. *The American Common School: An Historic Conception.* New York: Teachers College Press, 1951.

Crow, Tracy M. "The Necessity of Diversity." *Journal of Staff Development* 29, no.1 (Winter, 2008): 54-58.

Cruickshank, Donald, Deborah Jenkins, and Kim Metcalf. *The Act of Teaching.* 4th ed. Boston: McGraw-Hill, 2007.

Cummins, James. "Negotiating Identities: Education for Empowerment in a Diverse Society." *California Association for Bilingual Education,* Ontario, CA, 1996.

D'Angelo, Raymond. *Taking Sides—Clashing Views in Race and Ethnicity, 6th ed.* Dubuque, Iowa: McGraw-Hill, 2008.

Darling-Hammond Land J. Bransford. *Preparing Teachers for a Changing World: What Teachers Should Learn and Be Able to Do.* San Francisco: Jossey Bass, 2005.

Delpit, Lisa. *Other Peoples Children: Cultural Conflict in the Classroom.* New York: The New Press, 1995.

Dewey, John. *Experience and Education.* New york: MacMillan/Collier, 1938.

Doyle, W. "Classroom Organization and Management." In M. Wittrock, ed. *Handbook of Research on Teaching, 3rd ed.* 392-431. New York: Macmillan, 1986.

Doyle, W. *Classroom Management Techniques in O. C. Moles (Ed.), Student Discipline Strategies: Research and Practice.* Albany State University of New York Press, 1990.

Du Bois, W.E.B. *The Souls of Black Folk.* New York: Penguin Books, USA, Inc., 1961.

Duffy, T. and D. Cunningham. "Constructivism: Implications for the Design and Delivery of Instruction." D. Jonassen, ed. *Handbook of Research for Educational Communications and Technology.* New York: Macmillan, 1996.

Duit, R. "Students Conceptual Frameworks: Consequences for Learning in Science." In S. M. Glynn, R. H. Yeany, &B. K. Britton (Eds.), *The Psychology of Learning Science.* Hillsdale, NJ: Erlbaum, 1991.

Eby, Judy. *Reflective Planning, Teaching, and Evaluation for the Elementary School.* New York: Prentice Hall, 2001.

Edmonds, Ronald R. A Discussion of the Literature and Issues Related to Effective Schooling. Cambridge, MA: Center for Urban Studies, Harvard Graduate School of Education, 1979a.

Edmonds, Ronald R. *Making Public Schools Effective.* Social Policy 12 (2), 1981.

Eisenhower, J. S. D. *So Far from God: The U.S. War with Mexico 1846-1848.* New York: Anchor Books, 1989.

Eisner, Eliot. W. *The Educational Imagination: On the Design and Evaluation of School Programs (3rd ed.).* New York: Macmillan, 1994.

Emmer, Edmond T. and Carolyn Evertson. Teacher's Manual for the Junior High Classroom Management Improvement Study. Austin: R&D Center for Teacher Education, University of Texas, 1981.

Emmer, Edmond T. and Carolyn Evertson. *Classroom Management for Middle and High School Teachers, 8th ed..* New Jersey: Pearson, 2009.

Fisher, C., D. Berliner, N. Filby, R. Marliave, L. Cahen, and M. Dishaw. "Teaching Behaviors, Academic Learning Time, and Student Achievement: An Overview." In C. Denham and Lieberman (Eds.), *Time to Learn.* Washington D.C.: Dept of Education, 1980.

Epstein, Joyce L. & M. G. Sanders. "Family, School, and Community Partnerships." In M. Bornstein (Ed.), *Handbook of Parenting (2nd ed.).* Mahwah, NJ: Lawrence Erlbaum, 2002.

Francis, Paul P. *The Great Father: The United States Government and the American Indians.* Lincoln: University Press, 1984.

Freire, Paolo. *Pedagogy of the Oppressed.* New York: Continuum, 1970.

Freire, Paolo. *Education for Critical Consciousness.* New York: Continuum, 1973.

Freire Paolo. *Literacy, Reading the Word and World.* South Hadley, MN: Bergin and Grady, 1987.

Garcia, E. *Student Cultural Diversity: Understanding and Meeting the Challenge, 2nd ed.* Boston: Houghton Mifflin, 1999.

Gardner, Howard. *Frames of Mind: The Theory of Multiple Intelligences.* New York: Basic Books, 1993.

Gay, Geneva, ed., *Becoming Multicultural Educators.* Hoboken, New Jersey: John Wiley and Sons, 2003.

Genovese, Eugene D. *Roll Jordan Roll: The World the Slaves Made.* New York: Vintage Books, 1972.

Geertz, C. *The Interpretation of Cultures.* New York: Basic Books, 1973.

Giroux, Henry. A. *Teachers as Intellectuals: Toward a Critical Pedagogy of Learning.* Granby, Mass.: Bergin and Garvey Publishers, Inc., 1988.

Giroux, Henry. A. *Resisting Difference: Cultural Studies and the Discourse of Critical Pedagogy.* Philadelphia: Routledge, 1992.

Glasser, William. *The Quality School.* New York: Harper and Row Publishers, 1990.

Gollnick, Donna M. and Phillip C. Chinn. *Multicultural Education in a Pluralistic Society.* Pearson: New Jersey, 2006.

Gonzalez, Gilbert. *Chicano Education in the Era of Segregation.* Philadelphia: Balch Institute Press, 1990.

Good, Thomas and T. Beckerman. "Time on Task: A Naturalistic Study in Sixth Grade Classrooms," *The Elementary School Journal.* (1978) 78, 193-201.

Good, Thomas L. and Jere E. Brophy. *Looking in Classrooms, 8th ed.* New York: Addison Wesley Longman, Inc., 2000.

Goodlad, John. *A Place Called School, 20th Anniversary ed.* New York: McGraw-Hill, 2004.

Grant, Carl, ed. *Research and Multicultural Education: From the Margins to the Mainstream.* London: The Palmer Press, 1992.

Grant, Carl, and Maureen Gillette. *Learning to Teach Everyone's Children.* California: Thomson Wadsworth, 2006.

Guadalupe, San Miguel, Jr. *Let All of Them Take Heed: Mexican Americans and the Campaign for Educational Equality in Texas, 1910-1981.* Austin: University of Texas Press, 1987.

Gunstone, R. F., and R. T. White. "Understanding of Gravity," *Science Education.* 1981, 65, 291-299.

Hall, Edward T. *The Silent Language.* Greenwich, Ct.: Fawcett, 1959.

Harris, Ian, M. "Peace Education in a Violent Culture." *Harvard Educational Review* 77, no.3 (Fall, 2007): 350-354.

Hartzopovlos, Maria. "Deepening Democracy: How One School's Fairness Committee Offers an Alternative to Discipline," *Rethinking Schools*, 21, no.1 (Fall, 2006): 42-43.

Helms, J. "Why Is There No Study of Cultural Equivalence in Standardized Cognitive Ability Testing?" *American Psychologist.* 47, 9, (1992): 1083-1101.

Hirsch, E..D. Jr. *Cultural Literacy.* New York: Vintage Books, 1987.

Hofstede, Geert. *Culture's Consequence: International Differences in Work-Related Values.* Beverly Hills, CA: Sage, 1984.

Hunter, Madeline. *Mastery Teaching.* Thousand Oaks, CA: Corwin Press, 1982.

Jackson Lears, Thomas J. *No Place of Grace: Anti Modernism and the Transformation of American Culture 1880-1920.* University of Missouri Press, Columbia Missouri, 1981.

Jacobs, H.H. *Mapping the Big Picture: Integrating Curriculum and Assessment K-12.* Alexandria Virginia: Association for Supervision and Curriculum Development, 1997.

Hom, A, & V. Battistich. "Students' Sense of School Community as a Factor in Reducing Drug Use and Delinquency." Paper Presented at the Annual Meeting of the American Educational Research Association, San Francisco, 1995.

Joshi, Arti, Jody Eberly, & Jean Konzal. "Dialogue Across Cultures: Teachers' Perceptions About Communication with Diverse Families." *Multicultural Education.* 13, no. 2 (December, 2005):11-15.

Johnson, David W. and Roger T. Johnson. *Circles of Learning: Cooperation in the Classroom, 5th ed.* Arlington, Virginia: Association for Supervision and Curriculum Development, 1984.

Kaestle, Carl F. *Pillars of the Republic: Common Schools and American Society 1780-1860.* New York: Hill and Wang, 1983.

Kim, D, D. Solomon, & W. Roberts. "Classroom Practices That Enhance Students Sense of Community." Paper Presented at the Annual Meeting of the American Educational Research Association, San Francisco, 1995.

Kimball, S. T. *Culture and the Educative Process.* New York: Teachers College Press, 1974.

Klopf, Donald W. *Intercultural Encounters: The Fundamentals of Intercultural Communication.* Englewood, Co.: Morton Publishing Co., 1991.

Kohlberg, Lawrence. "Essays on Moral Development." *The Psychology of Moral Development.* 2. New York: Harper and Row, 1984.

Kohlberg, Lawrence. *The Psychology of Moral Development: The Nature and Validity of Moral Stages.* San Francisco: Harper and Rowe, 1984.

Kohn, Alfie. *Punished by Rewards.* New York: Houghton Mifflin Co., 1993.

Kounin, Jacob. *Group Management in Classrooms.* New York: Holt, Rinehart, Winston, Inc., 1970.

Kozol, Jonathan. *The Night is Dark and I am Far from Home.* New York: Simon and Schuster, 1975.

Kuhn, D., E. Amsel, & M. O'Loughlin. *The Development of Scientific Thinking Skills.* San Diego, Academic Press, 1988.

Ladson-Billings, Gloria. *The Dream Keepers: Successful Teachers of African American Children.* San Francisco: Jossey Bass, 1994.

Ladson-Billings, Gloria. "Preparing Teachers for Diverse Populations: A Critical Race Theory Perspective." In A, Iran-Nejd & P.D. Pearson (Eds.), *Review of Research in Education,* 24. Washington, D.C. American Educational Research Association, 1999.

Lansford, Jennifer. "Educating American Students for Life in a Global Society." *Center for Child and Family Policy* 2, no.4 (2002): 1-3.

Lee, James L., Charles J. Pulvino, and Philip A. Perrone. *Restoring Harmony, A Guide to Managing Schools.* Upper Saddle River, New Jersey: Prentice Hall, 1998.

Lee, Robert G. Orientals: *Asian Americans in Popular Culture.* Philadelphia: Temple University Press, 1999.

Lee, Seungyoun, and Mary Ellen Dallman. "Engaging in a Reflective Examination about Diversity: Interviews with Three Pre-service Teachers." *Multicultural Education.* 15, no. 4 (July 1, 2008): 36-44.

Lemann, Nicholas. *The Promised Land: The Great Black Migration and How It Changed America.* New York: Vintage Books, 1991.

Levine, Lawrence W. *Black Culture and Black Consciousness: African American Folk Thought from Slavery to Freedom.* New York: Oxford University Press, 1977.

Likona, Thomas. *Educating for Character.* New York: Bantam Books, 1991.

Likona, Thomas. *Raising Good Children: From Birth Through the Teen Age Years.* New York: Bantam Books, 1983.

Manning, M. L. and L. G. Baruth. *Multicultural Education of Children and Adolescents.* Boston: Allyn and Bacon, 2004.

Marx, Sherry, and Julie Pennington. "Pedagogies of Critical Race Theory: Experimentations with White Preservice Teachers." *Qualitative Studies in Education.* 16, no. 1 (2003): 91-110.

Marzano, Robert J., Debra J. Pickering, and J. McTighe. *Assessing Student Outcomes: Performance Assessment Using the Dimensions of Learning Model.* McREL Institute. Aurora, CO, 1993.

Marzano, Robert J. *What Works in Schools: Translating Research into Action.* Alexandria, VA: Association for Supervision and Curriculum Development, 2002-2003.

McEwan, Barbara. *The Art of Classroom Management: Effective Practices for Building Learning Communities.* Upper Saddle River, NJ: Prentice Hall, 2000.

McGreal, Thomas. *Successful Teacher Evaluation.* Alexandria, VA: Association for Supervision and Curriculum Development. 1983.

McLaren, Peter. *Life in Schools: An Introduction in the Foundations of Education, 5th ed.* Los Angeles: Pearson, 2007.

McLaughlin, W. G. *Cherokee Renascence in the New Republic.* Princeton: University of Princeton Press, 1986.

Ming, Kavin and Charles Dukes. "Fostering Cultural Competence Through School-Based Routines." *Multicultural Education* 14, no.1 (Fall, 2006): 42-49.

Mitchell, Diana. *Children's Literature, An Invitation to the World.* Boston, MA: Allyn and Bacon, 2003.

Monroe, Carla. "Understanding the Discipline Gap through a Cultural Lens: Implications for the Education of African American Students." *Intercultural Education* 16, no. 4 (October, 2005): 317-330.

Moore, John H. *The Emergence of the Cotton Kingdom in the Old Southwest: Mississippi 1770-1860.* Baton Rouge: Louisiana State University Press, 1988.

Nieto, Sonia. *Affirming Diversity: The Sociopolitical Context of Multicultural Education.* New York: Addison Wesley Longman, 2000.

Noddings, Nell. *The Challenge to Care in Schools: An Alternative Approach to Education.* New York: Teachers College Press, 1992.

Noddings, Nell. "Competence and Caring As Central to Teacher Education." Paper presented at the Annual meeting of the American Research Association. Montreal, 1999.

Noddings, Nell, ed. *Educating Citizens for Global Awareness.* New York: Teachers College Press, 2005.

Noddings, Nell. "Teaching the Themes of Care." *Phi Delta Kappan,* 76, (1995): 675-679.

Nuhlicek, Allan. "Relationship of School Boundary Conditions, Gemeinschaft Conditions, and Student Achievement Scores in Reading and Mathematics in Selected Milwaukee Public Schools." Ph.D. diss., Marquette University. Milwaukee, Wisconsin, 1981.

Oakes, Jeannie. *Keeping Track: How Schools Structure Inequality.* New Haven, CT: Yale University Press, 1999.

Oakes, Jeannie and Martin Lipton. *Teaching to Change the World (2nd ed.).* Boston: McGraw-Hill, 2003.

Obeakor, Festus E.. *It Even Happens in Good Schools: Responding to Cultural Diversity In Today's Classrooms.* CA: Corwin Press, 2001.

Ogbu, John. "Cultural Discontinuities and Schooling," *Anthropology and Education Quarterly*, 13, no.4, (1982): 290-307.

Ogbu, John. *Minority Status and Schooling: A Comparative Study of Immigrant and Involuntary Minorities.* New York: Garland, 1991.

Ogbu, John. "Understanding Cultural Diversity and Learning." *Educational Researcher* 21, no.8 (1992): 5-14.

Pai, Y., S. Adler, and L. K. Shadiow. *Cultural Foundations of Education.* Upper Saddle River: Pearson Education, Inc., 2006.

Pai, Y. S., and D. Pemberton. *Findings on Korean American Early Adolescents and Adolescents.* University of Missouri: Kansas City MO, 1987.

Palincsar, A. and A. Brown. "Reciprocal Teaching of Comprehension Monitoring Activities." *Cognition and Instruction* 2 (1984): 117-175.

Perkins, David and T. Blythe. "Putting Understanding Up Front." *Educational Leadership* 51, no. 4 (1992): 4-7.

Perrone, V. ed. *Expanding Student Assessment.* Alexandria, VA: Association for Supervision and Curriculum Development, 1991.

Pewewardy, C. "Learning Styles of American Indian/Alaska Native Students: A Review of Literature and Implications for Practice." *Journal of American Indian Education*, 41 (3), 22-56.

Piaget, Jean. *The Child's Conception of the World.* New York: Harcourt Brace, 1929.

Piaget, Jean. *Origins of Intelligence in Children.* New York: International Universities Press, 1952.

Pickett, Linda. "Diversity Education: Respect, Equality, and Social Justice." *Childhood Education* 84, no. 3 (Spring, 2008): 158.

Power, F.Clark, Ann Higgins, and Lawrence Kohlberg. *Lawrence Kohlberg's Approach to Moral Education.* New York: Columbia University Press, 1989.

Ravitch, Diane. *The Troubled Crusade: American Education, 1945-1980.* New York: Basic Books, 1983.

Ray, Katie. W. "Reading Aloud: Filling the Room with the Sound of Wondrous Words," *Wondrous Words: Writers and Writing in the Elementary Classroom.* NCTE, 1999.

Redfield, Robert. "The Contribution of Anthropology to the Education of Teachers." In F. A. J. Ianni & E. Storey (Eds.) *Cultural Relevance and Educational Issues,* (153-159). Boston: Little, Brown, 1973.

Resnick, Lauren. *Education and Learning to Think.* Washington D.C.: National Academy Press, 1987.

Resnick, Lauren. and I. Klopfer. "Toward the Thinking Curriculum: An Overview." In Resnick and Kloepfer, eds. *Toward the Thinking Curriculum: Current Cognitive Research.* (1989): 1-18.

Reyhner, J., and J. Eder. *American Indian Education: A History.* Norman OK: University of Oklahoma Press, 2004.

Rosenshine, Barak. "How Time Is Spent in Elementary Schools." In C. Denham and A. Lieberman, eds. *Time to Learn.* Washington, D.C.: Department of Education, 1980.

Rosenshine, Barak. "Teaching Functions in Instructional Programs." *The Elementary School Journal,* 83, (1983): 335-351.

Rowe, Mary B. "Wait Time, Slowing Down May be A Way of Speeding Up." *American Educator* 11, (Spring, 1987): 38-43, 47.

Shor, Ira. *Empowering Education: Critical Teaching for Social Change.* Chicago: University of Chicago Press, 1992.

Shor, Ira., and Paolo Freire. *A Pedagogy for Liberation: Dialogues on Transforming Education.* South Hadley, MA: Bergin & Garvey, 1987.

Short, Kathy G., Kathryn Pierce, and Mitchell Pierce, eds. *Talking About Books: Creating Literate Communities,* Portsmouth, New Hampshire: Heinemann Educational Books, 1990.

Sizer, Theodore. *Horace's Compromise: The Dilemma of the American High School.* Boston: Houghton-Mifflin, 1984.

Skinner, B. F. *Science and Human Behavior.* New York: Macmillan, 1953.

Sleeter, Christine, ed. *Empowerment through Multicultural Education.* New York: State University of New York Press, 1991.

Smith, Rogers. *Civic Ideals: Conflicting Visions of Citizenship in U. S. History.* New Haven: Yale University Press, 1997.

Sokolower, Jody. "Bringing Globalization Home, A High School Teacher Helps Immigrant Students Draw on Their Own Expertise." *Rethinking Schools,* 21, no.1 (Fall, 2006): 46-48.

Spindler, G. and I Spindler. *The American Cultural Dialogue and Its Transmission.* New York: Palmer Press, 1990.

Spindler, G. D., "Education in a Transforming America." In G. D. Spindler (Ed.), *Education and Culture* (132-147). New York: Holt, Reinhart, and Winston, 1963.

Spring, Joel. *The American School 1642-2004.* New York: McGraw-Hill, 2005.

Spring, Joel. *Conflict of Interests: The Politics of American Education.* New York: McGraw-Hill, 2005.

Spring, Joel. *Deculturalization and the Struggle for Equality: Dominated Cultures in the United States, 5th ed.* New York: McGraw Hill, 2006.

Stein, S. J. The Culture of Education Policy. New York: Teachers College Policy, 2005.

Stokes, Sandra. "A Partnership for Creating a Multicultural Teaching Force: A Model for the Present." *Multicultural Education* 7, no.1 (Fall, 1999): 8-12.

Strong, R. W., Silver. H.F., and Perini, M.J. *Teaching What Matters Most: Standards and Strategies for Raising Student Achievement.* Alexandria, VA: Association for Supervision and Curriculum Development, 2001.

Takaki, Ronald. *A Different Mirror: A History of Multicultural America.* Boston: Little Brown and Company, 1993.

Taylor, George R., ed. *Practical Applications of Classroom Management Theories into Strategies.* Dallas: University Press of America, 2004.

Thompson, Gail L. *The Power of One: How You Can Help or Harm African American Students.* CA: Corwin Press, 2010.

Tyler, Ralph. *Basic Principles of Curriculum and Instruction.* Chicago: University of Chicago Press, 1949.

Vang, Christopher T. "Minority Parents Should Know More about School Culture and Its Impact on Their Children's Education." *Multicultural Education.* 14, no. 3 (April 1, 2007): 32-40.

Vygotsky, Lev S. *Mind in Society: The Development of Higher Psychological Processes.* Cambridge, MA: Harvard University Press, 1978.

Wang, M.C., G.D. Haertel & H.J. Wahlberg "What Helps Students Learn?" *Educational Leadership*, (1993/1994) 51(4), 74-79.

Whitehead, Alfred N. *The Aims of Education and Other Essays.* New York: Free Press, 1929.

Wiggins, Grant. "Practicing What We Preach in Designing Authentic Assessment." *Educational Leadership*, 54, 4 (1996-1997): 18-25.

Wiggins, Grant & Jay McTighe. *Understanding by Design.* Arlington, VA: Association for Supervision and Curriculum Development, 1998.

Wink, Joan. *Critical Pedagogy: Notes from the Real World.* Boston: Pearson, 2005.

Wong, Harry K. and Rosemary T. Wong. *The First Days of School.* California: Harry T. Wong Publications, 1998.

Zinn, Howard. *A Peoples History of the United States 1492-Present.* New York: Harper Collins, 1999.

# Advanced Praise for MASS Professional Development Series

Many of the concepts and principles expressed throughout this Professional Development series were initiated at Bruce-Guadalupe Community School where Dr. Newsome provided consultant services over a five year period to our culturally diverse Latino-American school. The practices were well received by the faculty, community, and students as we opened a new culturally-enriched schooling opportunity for students in the Milwaukee, Wisconsin community. We continue to be grateful to Dr. Newsome for her dedicated work. Readers should find the program which she has outlined in this series to be thoughtful, insightful and practical.

—Walter Sava, Ph.D. Executive Director, Bruce-Guadalupe Community School. Milwaukee, WA

The culturally-centered approach to classroom practice which Dr. Newsome has undertaken in this series is a progressive step forward in pre service and graduate study for our schools of education. It is time to move past the dominant-culture mindset. I agree that we all too often take on the status quo rather than challenging our assumptions and broadening our perspectives about cultures beyond our own. This series is definitely needed in education and beyond.

—Elaine Roberts, Ph.D., Professor, University of West Georgia. Carrollton, GA

Dr. Newsome's unique perspective and approach to classroom practice has been a source of enrichment for me. As a faculty member who worked closely with Dr. Newsome in developing and implementing a key component of this professional development series, I have broadened and systematically incorporated the culturally-transformative approach to teaching in my work with students and into my own teaching repertoire. Readers are sure to change their practices as a result of reading and engaging with the ideas in this series.

—Cathleen Doheny, Ph.D., Professor, Edison State College, Edison, FL

Dr. Newsome's ideas are enlightening to educators everywhere. What I like most about the book series is that it not only covers standard classroom practice, she takes it a step further to discuss how to prepare teachers to operate in a culturally diverse world. She breaks the information down bit by bit in a way that it is extremely understandable to her readers. Her book series is one of my most valuable purchases. I recommend reading it and keeping it as a refresher.

—Mallori Saylor, Student, University of West Georgia, Carrollton, GA

www.ingramcontent.com/pod-product-compliance
Lightning Source LLC
Chambersburg PA
CBHW080550170426
43195CB00016B/2736